To Micheline, with love and thanks for gifting me your childhood Barbie and friends.

Also by Linda Wright

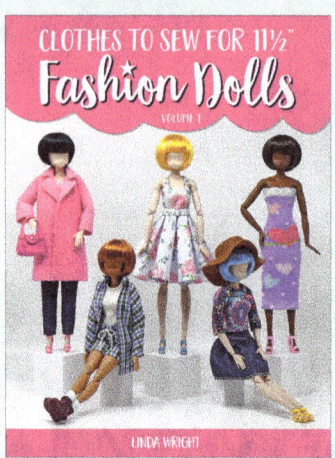

**Clothes to Sew for 11 1/2 Inch Fashion Dolls
Volume 1**

Credits
Photography: Linda and Randy Wright

All rights reserved. No part of this book may be reproduced, stored in a retrieval system, or transmitted, in any form or by any means, electronic, mechanical, photocopying, recording, or otherwise, without prior written permission from the publisher. Permission is granted to photocopy patterns and templates for the personal use of the retail purchaser.

Copyright © 2025 Linda Wright
Edition 1

Lindaloo Enterprises
Santa Barbara, California
United States

ISBN: 978-1-937564-20-9

CONTENTS

INTRODUCTION   4
Fashion Doll Measurements   6
Fabric   6
Tips & Tools   7
General Directions   8

GARMENT GALLERY and SEWING INSTRUCTIONS

Graffiti Jacket, Tutu Skirt & Bustier   11
Halter Dress   13
Breezy Tank & 4-Tier Skirt   15
Candy Stripe Dress & Santa Hat   19
Frilled Camisole & Skirt   21
Power Suit   23
T-Shirt Dress   25
Fingerless Gloves & Footless Stockings   25
Ruffle-Trim Blouse & Full Skirt   27
Scrubs   29
Cargo Capri Pants & Short-Sleeve Top   31
V-Neck Day Dress   33
Shell, Infinity Scarf & Pencil Pants   35
Hooded Cape   37
Hi-Lo Coat & Column Gown   39
Fringe Dress   41
Tent Dress & Bucket Bag   43
Turtleneck Shirt & Straight Skirt   45
Fringe Belt, Bra Top & Jeans Shorts   47
Friendship Bracelet & Inspiration Necklace   49
Bow Maxi Dress   51
Boat-Neck Top & Palazzo Pants   53
Pajamas, Slippers & Sleep Mask   55
Cap-Sleeve Crop Top & Wide-Leg Pants   57
Sweater Dress & Hat   59
Open-Front Jacket & Flare-Leg Jeans   61
Ruched Purse   62

FULL-SIZE PATTERNS   63

ABOUT THE AUTHOR   127

INTRODUCTION

Welcome to my second book of garments and accessories for 11½" fashion dolls! In this volume, you will find patterns for a well-rounded wardrobe — with items that can be mixed-and-matched into countless outfits.

The tops in this collection include a bra style, bustier, tank top, crop top, sleeveless, cap-sleeves, short-sleeves and long-sleeves. Pants include shorts, capris, narrow legs, wide legs and flares. Skirts range from mini to maxi and dresses from casual to fancy. You will also find career clothes, nightwear, outerwear and a festive holiday outfit.

These patterns are designed to be cute outfits that sewists of any level can make. Most sleeves are *cut on*, eliminating the need to *set in* a tiny sleeve. The most fiddly part of constructing 1/6-scale doll clothes is hemming a round neckline, but an all-purpose glue stick can make this step this much easier. Using specialty materials such as faux leather and sequin fabric elevates simple styles. Even by choosing quilt-weight cotton in a classy animal print, you can add instant sophistication!

If you are new to sewing, or unfamiliar with certain techniques, YouTube.com offers a wide assortment of excellent video tutorials. Beginners can watch the fundamentals of pinning and cutting pattern pieces, machine sewing, and hand sewing. Demos of specific methods and products are plentiful, such as how to gather fabric; sew darts; turn narrow tubes right-side out; use a loop turner; sew on snaps; apply fusible tape; or alter a pattern. I have assembled a collection of my favorite educational sewing videos on Pinterest. You can view them at www.pinterest.com/LindalooEnt/ on a board named "Sewing Basics".

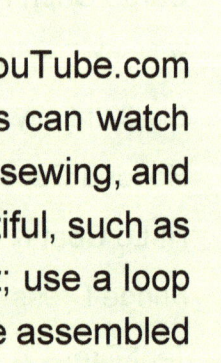

The standard seam allowance for these patterns is 1/4" (6mm). It is very important to be accurate since even a tiny variation can throw off the fit of such small-scale clothing. Note that most standard presser feet are wider than 1/4". If you align fabric with the edge of these feet, the garments will come out too small. A 1/4" (6mm) presser foot, sometimes called a quilting foot, is the way to achieve perfect 1/4" (6mm) seams.

All patterns are full-size and located at the back of the book. You can remove the pages for use, photocopy them or trace them.

Thank You for buying my book! If you enjoy my patterns, I would appreciate it so much if you post a brief review at your online place of purchase. Other customers would appreciate it too!

Happy Sewing!

Linda

FASHION DOLL MEASUREMENTS

These patterns are designed for the popular brand of 11½" fashion dolls. Measure your doll's body to compare with the measurements below. If adjustments are needed, allow for them when cutting fabric.

Size & Height.................................... 11 1/2" (29cm)
Bust.. 5" (13cm)
Outer leg length, waist to ankle .... 6 3/4" (17cm)
Waist.. 3 1/2" (9cm)
Hip .... 5" (13cm)
Scale.. 1:6

Patterns are made to fit measurements of 'original' body type Barbie® Made-to-Move™, Fashionista™ and Looks™ dolls.

FABRIC

Tightly-woven, lightweight, cotton fabrics — such as the cotton used for quilts, are the easiest materials to handle for sewing such small doll clothes. Fat Quarters are perfect. Thrift store garments to upcycle are another good source of material. Remember to check your closet for clothes you no longer wear or your giveaway pile. T-Shirt fabric works well when knits are needed. Baby clothes are excellent for cute little prints on thin fabric.

♥ **Pre-Shrinking.** New cotton yardage should be pre-shrunk before cutting. To pre-shrink by soaking: loosely fold the fabric, submerge in a sink of hot water for 30 minutes, drain water and gently press fabric with hands to remove moisture (do not wring). Machine dry or hang to dry.

The following **specialty fabrics** are used in this book. One makes sewing simpler, while the others add drama and shine. Read below for tips:

♥ **Felt.** Felt is fun because it doesn't fray and it's thick enough to create structure and shape. Be sure to use polyester felt for fashion doll clothes. Wool felt is beautiful, but it can shrink enough from pressing to make a garment too small for your doll.

♥ **Faux Leather.** Also called Leatherette or Pleather. Comes in 2 main types, **Non-Stretch** and **Stretch** (with spandex). Both types are sold on Amazon and Etsy.

Non-stretch is sold in pre-cut sheets for sewing and crafts. Use a size 14 standard needle, jeans needle or leather needle. **Stretch** is sold by the yard. Use a stretch needle to prevent skipped stitches.

Pins leave permanent holes in all faux leather! Only use pins in seam allowances. Hold patterns in place with tape for cutting. Secure pieces with mini clips or your fingers for sewing. Do not press directly with an iron. Always use a press cloth and test first on scraps.

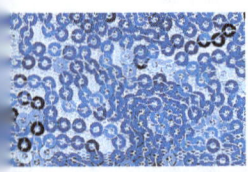

♥ **Sequin Fabric.** Sequin fabric with small scattered sequins (not overlapping) is best for doll-sized garments. I bought the fabric pictured on Amazon. Use a stretch needle in your machine. To press, if needed, place iron on back side of fabric, use low heat and a press cloth. A lint roller or wide painter's tape works well to clean up scattered sequins from your work area.

♥ **Tulle.** This sheer, lightweight mesh fabric adds delicate layers and fullness to fashion doll clothes. Economical rolls, 6 inches wide, are perfect when a pattern calls for tulle.

TIPS & TOOLS

♥ **All-Purpose Scissors**: For cutting out paper patterns. Small scissors are good for tight curves.

♥ **Dressmaker's Shears**: For cutting fabric.

♥ **Pinking Shears**: Can be used to trim seam allowances, after a seam is sewn, to prevent raveling, and to help them lay flatter.

♥ **Straight Pins**: For holding patterns to fabric and keeping materials together while you stitch. Thin pins are best for lightweight fabrics.

♥ **Sewing Machine Needles**: Small sizes (10 & 12) are best for the lightweight fabrics used for doll clothes. Ballpoint needles & stretch needles are key to success for sewing knits.

♥ **Loop Turner**: For turning narrow fabric cylinders and tubes right side out. Search *'how to use a loop turner'* on YouTube to see demo videos.

♥ **6" (15.2cm) Serrated-Tip Hobby Tweezers**: My go-to for turning pant legs, long sleeves and stockings right side out. Insert tweezers in tunnel, pinch tips on seam allowance and pull through.

♥ **Seam Gauge**: A measuring tool with a sliding marker that stays in place. Very helpful when pressing under narrow hems and casings.

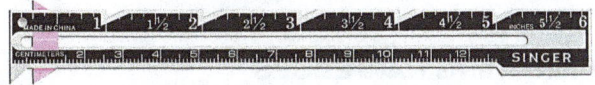

♥ **1/4" (6mm) Presser Foot**: A sewing machine accessory for making accurate 1/4" (6mm) seams. My *clear plastic* 1/4" (6mm) presser foot was a true game changer, providing clear visibility of the fabric under the foot. This makes it much easier to precisely place stitches on the tight curves of tiny garments. Note — Most standard presser feet are wider than 1/4". Don't line up fabric with the edge of this presser foot or the garments will come out too small.

♥ **Disappearing Ink Marking Pen**: For making non-permanent marks on fabric such as darts, dots and other pattern symbols.

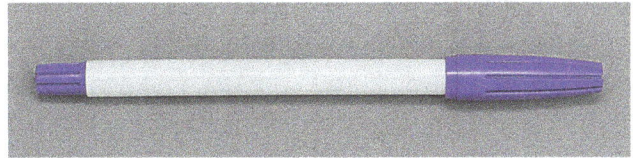

♥ **Tailor's Chalk**: For marking dark fabrics. My sewing box includes 3 types: triangular tailor's chalk, a chalk pencil and a chalk wheel.

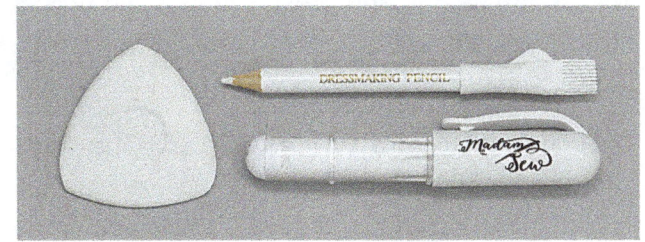

♥ **Glue:** Fabri Tac® is an excellent fabric glue that can be a great aid for attaching straps & adornments. I use an Avery Glue Stic™ for securing turned necklines or sleeveless armholes prior to topstitching. Always test on your fabric first!

♥ **Velcro®**: Sew-on hook-&-loop fastener tape used for closures. Easy for children to manipulate. My favorite for doll clothes is Velcro® Sleek & Thin™. This type is no-snag and won't get tangled in doll hair.

♥ **Snaps**: Closures made from metal or plastic. Can be substituted for Velcro®, if desired.

♥ **Elastic**: Elastic is manufactured as braided or knit. For doll clothes, get *braided*. This provides a firmer hold that stays strong over time.

♥ **Tissue Paper or Wax Paper**: Use under delicate fabric when machine sewing to prevent it from being pulled down into the needle plate. Easy to tear off after. For best results, use a small stitch length.

♥ **Cutting Board**: A folding cardboard cutting board laid on a bed makes a great cutting table and stores compactly! Dritz and Singer make them.

♥ **Thread Dish**: I use a ceramic bowl near my sewing machine to collect the thread tails trimmed off seams while sewing.

GENERAL DIRECTIONS

♥ **SEAM ALLOWANCE** - Patterns include seam allowances. Seam allowances are 1/4" (6mm) unless instructions indicate otherwise. Applicable patterns will indicate a 1/2" (1.2cm) seam allowance at center back to allow extra fabric for fitting the garment to your doll: You can sew that seam with a smaller seam allowance if needed for a good fit. Sometimes small adjustments are needed just because of the properties of the fabric being used.

♥ **STITCH** - With RIGHT sides together, sew 1/4" (6mm) seams and press seams open unless otherwise indicated.

♥ **RIGHT SIDE and WRONG SIDE** - The "right side" of the fabric is meant to be visible from the outside of your garment for everyone to see, while the "wrong side" is the side that will be hidden on the inside of the garment.

♥ **CLIP CURVES or NOTCH CURVES** - When a seam is curved, turning the fabric right side out can cause pulling or wrinkling. To make curved seams lay flat, use the tips of your shears to **clip** or **notch** the seam allowance, taking care not to cut into the stitching.

• **Inner Curve** - Cut small slits or **CLIPS**.

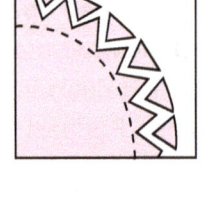

• **Outer Curve** - Cut small V-shaped **NOTCHES**.

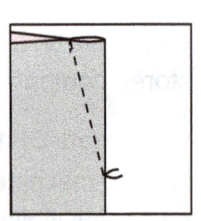

♥ **DARTS** - With RIGHT sides of fabric together, bring dotted lines of darts together. Sew along dotted lines from wide end to point.

♥ **GATHER** - Sew along the 1/4" (6mm) seamline and 1/8" (3mm) away in the seam allowance, using a long machine stitch.

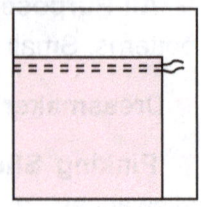

♥ **TRIM OUTER CORNER** - Cut off excess seam allowance at point of corner and at each side.

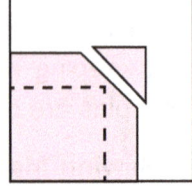

♥ **CLIP INNER CORNER** - Cut a slit into the corner.

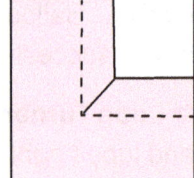

♥ **BACKSTITCHING** - Backstitch at beginning and end of all seams to secure stitching. To backstitch, put machine in reverse and stitch again over previous stitching for about 1/2" (1.3cm).

♥ **STAYSTITCHING** - A reinforcement stitch. Stitch on the stitchline, thru one layer of fabric, with a slightly smaller stitch than normal.

♥ **TOPSTITCHING** - Decorative stitching on the outside of a garment, usually with a straight stitch.

♥ **FINISHING RAW EDGES**

To prevent raveling and make the inside of a garment look nice, raw edges may be finished with pinking shears, a zigzag stitch, serger or Fray Check fabric sealant.

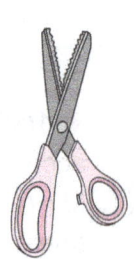

♥ **SPAGHETTI STRAP TIP**

Several patterns include narrow straps. If you find them difficult to handle, try making 1 extra-long strap, then cut to size into 2 straps.

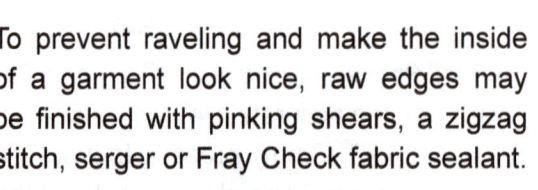

GENERAL DIRECTIONS

♥ FINISHING BACK OPENING EDGES

Use 3/4" wide (19mm) Velcro. If your Velcro includes smooth "sewing lanes" along the sides, cut them off before Step 3.

 RIGHT SIDE OF FABRIC    WRONG SIDE OF FABRIC

1. Press under 1/2" (1.2cm) on one side of back opening.

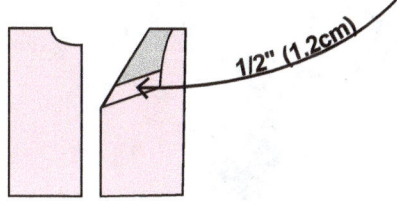

2. Cut a length of Velcro to fit opening.

3. Cut width of Velcro to make strip 3/8" (8mm) wide.

4. Separate halves of Velcro.

3/8" (8mm) wide — ROUGH SIDE / SOFT SIDE

5. Sew **rough side** of Velcro on INSIDE along pressed edge.

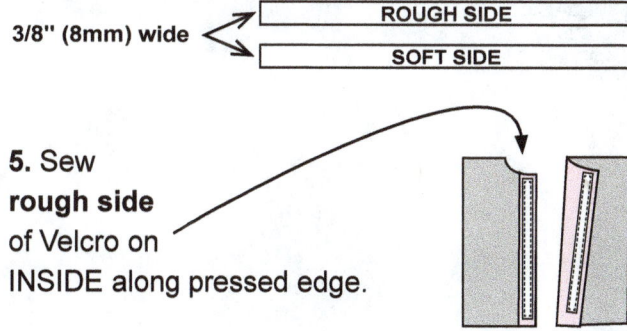

6. Sew **soft side** of Velcro on OUTSIDE of opposite back opening, having one long edge along **center back**, or as needed for best fit.

7. Press seam allowance to one side.

♥ INSERTING ELASTIC

Attach safety pin at end of elastic piece, then push pin into casing. You can feel the end of the safety pin and slide it forward, gathering up the fabric, then pulling the excess fabric back behind the pin. Work the safety pin through in this manner, inching it through the casing until it appears on the other end of the tunnel.

♥ PRESSING

Pressing as you sew is crucial for a professional outcome. Pressing sets stitches into the fabric, flattens seams for less bulk, makes seams less visible, and shapes the garment. To press your sewn pieces, lift the iron and place it gently down on a specific area, then lift it and move it again. It's an up-and-down motion rather than a side-to-side motion. I use a standard iron and ironing board for doll clothes, but small versions of both are available, if preferred.

Tip: To make a **Seam Roll** for pressing small cylinders such as pant legs and sleeves, roll a thin catalog or a piece of cardstock tightly. It will expand to fit the space perfectly.

♥ ALTERATIONS

If your fashion doll has slightly different proportions from the measurements on page 6, follow these tips.

• **Enlarge:** Add extra fabric at the side seams when you cut.

• **Reduce:** Sew with a slightly larger seam allowance to take in the fit.

• **Lengthen:** Before cutting the fabric, extend the pattern at the hem or sleeve edge by the desired amount.

• **Shorten:** Trim the hem or sleeve edge before sewing.

GRAFFITI JACKET

You can sew first, then write your graffiti on the completed jacket — or trace my graffiti on faux-leather before sewing. The jacket edges are left raw. To cut a smooth curve on the neckline, small scissors work best. See page 6 for tips about working with faux leather.

This pattern can be made from felt without graffiti.

SUPPLIES

Lightweight faux-leather fabric, 8" x 12" sheet
Sharpie permanent marker, fine tip

Note: PATTERN IS ON PAGE 65. Pattern includes seam allowances. Seam allowances are 1/4" (6mm) unless instructions indicate otherwise.

1. With RIGHT sides together, stitch front to back at entire underarm seam. Clip seam allowance at armpit. Trim seam allowances to 1/8" (3mm).

Note: Turning a faux leather sleeve right-side out can be tricky. Use long craft tweezers (see page 7). Get started by tucking end of sleeve to the inside as much as possible, about 1/2" (1cm). Slide in tweezers and pinch firmly on seam allowance and end of sleeve. Then work patiently, coaxing the sleeve on the outside with your fingers and pulling from the inside with the tweezers. ♥

TUTU SKIRT & BUSTIER

SUPPLIES

Lightweight cotton fabric, 1/8 yd (.11m)
Tulle, 1/4 yd (.23m) or 1 roll, 6" wide
Faux-leather or 1/8" (3mm) wide ribbon
3/4" (19mm) wide Velcro® Sleek & Thin™ sew-on tape
1 snap

Note: PATTERNS ARE ON PAGE 67. Pattern includes seam allowances. Seam allowances are 1/4" (6mm) unless instructions indicate otherwise.

TUTU SKIRT

The skirt has 4 layers of tulle and 1 layer of cotton.

1. Press under 1/4" (6mm) on lower edge of underskirt. Sew 1/8" (3mm) from pressed edge.

2. Stack the 4 tulle pieces on OUTSIDE of underskirt, having raw edges even. Pin in place. To gather upper edge, machine-baste 1/4" & 1/8" (6mm and 3mm) from edge thru all layers.

3. With RIGHT sides together, pin upper edge of skirt to WAISTBAND, matching centers and having edges even. Pull up bobbin threads and adjust gathers to fit. Stitch in place. Press seam toward waistband.

4. Press under 1/4" (6mm) on other long edge of waistband. Fold pressed edge over seam allowance to meet stitchline. Sew in place by hand with whip stitch.

5. With RIGHT sides together, pin center back seam of UNDERSKIRT ONLY, taking care that tulle layers are not caught in seam. Sew **1/2" (1.2cm)** from edge, stitching from hem to DOT (see pattern).

6. Turn under 1/2" (1.2cm) on one back opening edge. Sew prong half of snap to INSIDE on waistband. Sew socket half of snap to OUTSIDE on opposite edge. ♥

BUSTIER

1. Sew darts in BUSTIER. Press darts toward center.

2. To staystitch, sew 1/4" (6mm) from upper edge. Press under 1/4" (6mm) using stitchline for a guide, clipping to staystitching at center front. Sew 1/8" (3mm) from pressed edge.

3. Press under 1/4" (6mm) on lower edge. Sew 1/8" (3mm) from pressed edge.

4. For each strap, cut faux leather 1/8" x 2 1/4" (3 x 57mm) or use 1/8" wide (3mm) ribbon. Lap upper edge of bustier 3/8" (8mm) over straps at DOTS (see pattern). Sew in place.

5. Apply fastener; see FINISHING BACK OPENING EDGES, page 9, Steps 1-6. ♥

HALTER DRESS

The belt has a decorative knot at center front and a snap closure at the back. The dress can be worn without the belt for a different look.

SUPPLIES

Lightweight woven cotton fabric, 1/4 yd (.23m)
3/4" (19mm) wide Velcro® Sleek & Thin™ sew-on tape
2 snaps

Note: PATTERN IS ON PAGE 69. Pattern includes seam allowances. Seam allowances are 1/4" (6mm) unless instructions indicate otherwise.

1. With RIGHT sides together, stitch FRONT to BACK at side seams. Clip curves.

2. Press under 1/4" (6mm) on entire armhole edge. Sew 1/8" (3mm) from pressed edge.

3. For casing, press under 1/2" (1.2cm) on upper edge. Sew 3/8" (9mm) from pressed edge.

4. Press under 1/4" (6mm) on lower edge of RUFFLE. Sew 1/8" (3mm) from pressed edge.

5. To gather upper edge of ruffle, machine-baste 1/4" and 1/8" (6mm and 3mm) from raw edge.

6. With RIGHT sides together, pin ruffle to lower edge of dress, matching centers and having edges even. Pull up bobbin threads and adjust gathers to fit. Stitch in place. Press seam allowance toward dress. On OUTSIDE, topstitch dress 1/8" (3mm) from ruffle seam.

7. With RIGHT sides together, sew up center back, **1/2" (1.2cm)** from edge, stitching from hem to DOT (see pattern).

8. Press under 1/4" (6mm) on both long edges of NECK BAND & BELT pieces. Then fold in half lengthwise, WRONG sides together, and press again. Sew lengthwise along center thru all layers.

9. Using a small safety pin, insert neck band thru casing, gathering neckline tight, and having ends extend evenly. Turn under 1/4" (6mm) on one end of band. Sew prong half of snap to inside on this end. Sew socket half of snap to outside on opposite end.

10. Tie an overhand knot at center front of belt. Turn under 1/4" (6mm) on one end of belt. Sew prong half of snap to INSIDE of this end. Sew socket half of snap to OUTSIDE of opposite end.

11. Apply fastener; see FINISHING BACK OPENING EDGES, page 9. ♥

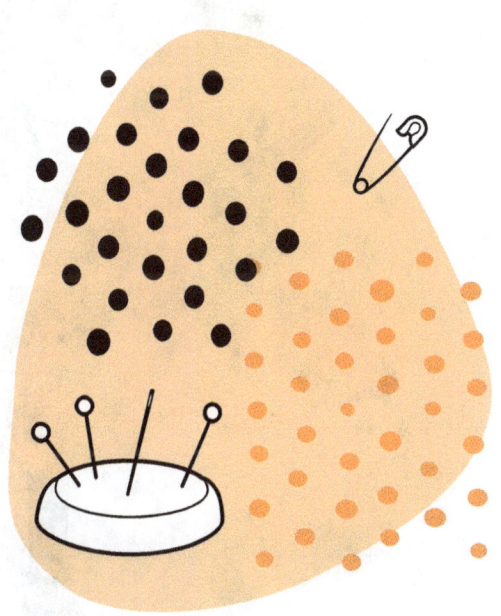

BREEZY TANK & 4-TIER SKIRT

The skirt is constructed with a technique that creates little ruffles between the tiers. Alternating solid and print fabrics adds definition to each tier.

Tip: Use a sticky note as a placeholder while sewing. Move it down each time a step is completed.

SUPPLIES

Lightweight cotton print fabric, 1/4 yd (.23m)
Lightweight cotton solid fabric, 1/8 yd (.11m)
3/4" (19mm) wide Velcro® Sleek & Thin™ sew-on tape
1/8" wide braided elastic

Note: PATTERNS ARE ON PAGE 71. Pattern includes seam allowances. Seam allowances are 1/4" (6mm) unless instructions indicate otherwise.

BREEZY TANK

1. Press under 1/4" (6mm) on upper edge of YOKE. Sew 1/8" (3mm) from pressed edge.

2. Press under 1/4" (6mm) lower edge of BODICE. Sew 1/8" (3mm) from pressed edge.

3. To gather upper edge of bodice, machine baste 1/4" and 1/8" (6mm and 3mm) from raw edge.

4. With RIGHT sides together, pin upper edge of bodice to yoke, matching centers & having edges even. Pull up bobbin threads & adjust gathers to fit. Stitch in place. Press seam toward yoke.

5. Press under 1/4" (6mm) on both long edges of STRAPS. Fold straps in half lengthwise, WRONG sides together and press again. Sew lengthwise along center of each strap thru all layers.

6. Lap upper edge of yoke 3/8" (9mm) over straps at DOTS (see pattern), being careful not to twist straps. Sew in place.

7. Apply fastener; see FINISHING BACK OPENING EDGES, page 9, Steps 1-6. ♥

4-TIER SKIRT

First you will piece strips together for Tiers 4 and 3.

1. To connect the 2 sections of TIER 4 into one 40" (100 cm) strip, pin RIGHT sides together with a short end of each strip aligned. Stitch.

2. Connect the 2 sections of TIER 3 in the same manner. Trim to 30" (76 cm) long & discard excess.

Next, the skirt is assembled from the bottom up.

3. Press under 1/4" (6mm) on both long edges of TIER 4. Sew 1/8" (3mm) from pressed edges

4. Machine baste TIER 4 on gathering line (see pattern).

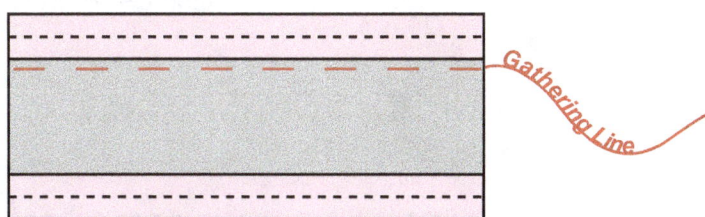

5. With RIGHT SIDES UP, pin TIER 4 to lower edge of TIER 3, matching centers and back edges, with gathering line along **seamline*** of TIER 3. Pull up bobbin threads and adjust gathers to fit. Sew on top of gathering stitches.

> ***Tip:** With a Disappearing Ink Marking Pen, draw a line 1/4" (6mm) from lower edge of Tier 3. Match this up with the gathering line of Tier 4 to pin in place. Repeat when connecting remaining tiers.*

6. Press under 1/4" (6mm) on top edge of TIER 3. Sew 1/8" (3mm) from pressed edge.

7. Machine baste TIER 3 on gathering line (see pattern).

8. With RIGHT SIDES UP, pin TIER 3 to lower edge of TIER 2, matching centers and back edges, with gathering line along seamline of TIER 2. Pull up bobbin threads and adjust gathers to fit. Sew on top of gathering stitches.

9. Press under 1/4" (6mm) on <u>top</u> edge of TIER 2. Sew 1/8" (3mm) from pressed edge.

10. Machine baste TIER 2 on gathering line (see pattern).

11. With RIGHT SIDES UP, pin TIER 2 to <u>lower</u> edge of TIER 1, matching centers and back edges, with gathering line along seamline of TIER 1. Pull up bobbin threads and adjust gathers to fit. Sew on top of gathering stitches.

12. For casing, press under 5/8" (15mm) on <u>top</u> edge of TIER 1. Sew 3/8" (9mm) from pressed edge.

13. Cut elastic 3 1/2" (9cm) long. Using a small safety pin, insert elastic thru casing and sew securely at ends.

14. With RIGHT sides together, stitch center back seam. ♥

FINISHING

To shape the flare of the garments, dress doll and lightly spray water on fabric. Compress into shape by squeezing with your hand into desired look. Let dry on doll. ♥

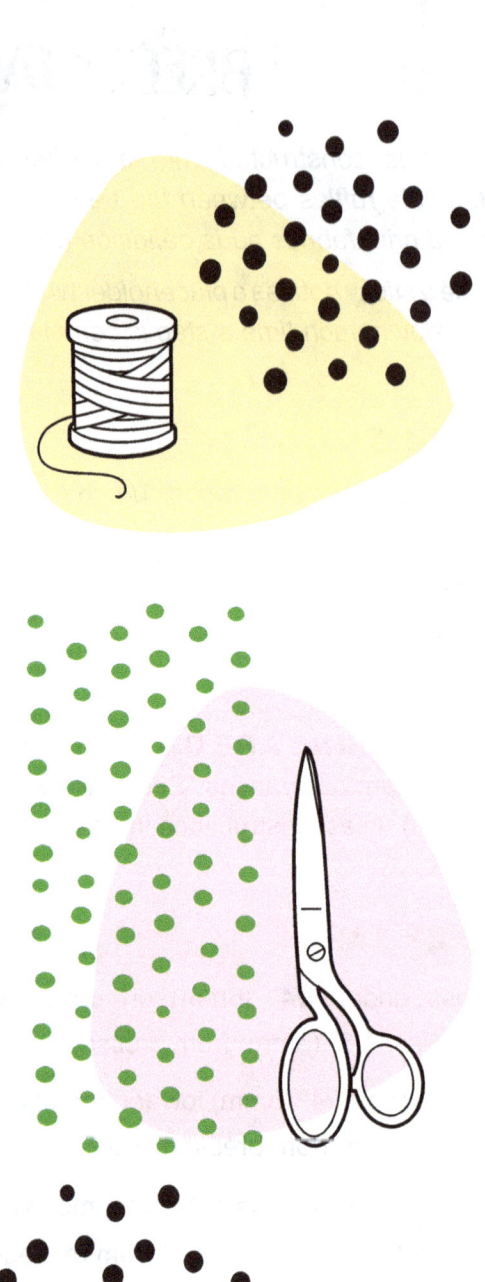

CANDY STRIPE DRESS

The festive Christmas dress captures the spirit of holiday confections with mini 1/8" red and white stripes. The style is fit-and-flare, cut in 1 piece. Vertical darts create the shapely silhouette.

The waist is cinched with a belt. A red & white striped paper clip is perfect for the buckle!

The outfit is pictured with Footless Stockings, pattern on page 25.

SUPPLIES

Lightweight woven or knit fabric, 3/8 yd (.34m)

3/4" (19mm) wide Velcro® Sleek & Thin™ sew-on tape

Felt or faux leather (belt)

Paper clip or 18 gauge craft wire; wire cutters & file

1/2" (1cm) diameter marking pen

All purpose glue stick, optional

Note: PATTERN IS ON PAGE 73. Pattern includes seam allowances. Seam allowances are 1/4" (6mm) unless instructions indicate otherwise.

1. To make darts, fold on solid line, RIGHT SIDES TOGETHER. Sew on dotted line. Press fold of darts toward center.

2. On neckline, stitch 1/4" (6mm) from edge. Press or glue* under on stitchline, clipping curves. Sew 1/8" (3mm) from turned edge. * Note: To glue, lightly dab glue stick along wrong side of seam allowance and finger-press in place.

3. Make clips in side seams at DOTS (see pattern). Press under 1/4" (6mm) between dots to create armholes. Sew 1/8" from pressed edge.

4. With RIGHT sides together, stitch front to back at side seams.

5. Press under 1/4" (6mm) on lower edge of dress. Sew 1/8" (3mm) from pressed edge.

6. With RIGHT sides together, sew up center back of dress **1/2" (1.2cm)** from edge, stitching from hem to DOT (see pattern).

7. Apply fastener; see FINISHING BACK OPENING EDGES, page 9.

8. For BELT and BUCKLE, follow instructions on page 23. ♥

SANTA HAT

If your faux fur is very plush, cut from wrong side of fabric, cutting only thru the backing.

SUPPLIES

9"x12" pre-cut polyester felt fabric, 1 piece

Faux fur fabric

Fabric glue

Note: PATTERN IS ON PAGE 73. Pattern includes seam allowances. Seam allowances are 1/4" (6mm) unless instructions indicate otherwise.

1. Pin RIGHT side of BRIM to WRONG side of HAT with lower edges aligned. Stitch. Trim seam allowance to 1/8" (3mm).

2. Turn brim to outside. Glue in place.

3. With RIGHT sides together, fold hat in half lengthwise so that edges meet. Stitch.

4. On POM POM, hand gather with running stitch 1/8" (3mm) from edge. Pull up gathers to form a cup, stuff with bits of fabric, then pull gathers tight. Secure with a knot. Sew pom pom to tip of hat. ♥

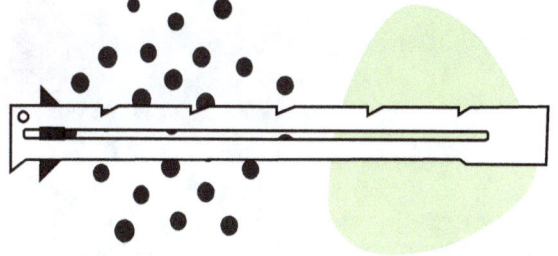

FRILLED CAMISOLE & SKIRT

Use contrasting thread as pictured. This outfit is also cute made from cotton print fabric.

Pictured with Bucket Bag, page 43.

SUPPLIES

Lightweight denim fabric, 1/8 yd (.11m)
3/4" (19mm) wide Velcro® Sleek & Thin™ sew-on tape

Note: PATTERNS ARE ON PAGE 75. Pattern includes seam allowances. Seam allowances are 1/4" (6mm) unless instructions indicate otherwise.

FRILLED CAMISOLE

1. Press under 1/4" (6mm) on upper edge of BODICE. Sew 1/8" (3mm) from pressed edge.

2. Press under 1/4" (6mm) on lower edge of RUFFLE. Sew 1/8" (3mm) from pressed edge.

3. To gather upper edge of ruffle, machine-baste 1/4" and 1/8" (6mm and 3mm) from raw edge.

4. With RIGHT sides together, pin ruffle to lower edge of bodice, matching centers and having edges even. Pull up bobbin threads and adjust gathers to fit. Stitch in place. Press seam allowance toward bodice. On OUTSIDE, topstitch bodice 1/8" (3mm) from ruffle seam.

5. Press under 1/4" (6mm) on both long edges of STRAPS. Fold straps in half lengthwise, WRONG sides together and press again. Sew lengthwise along center of each strap thru all layers.

6. Lap upper edge of bodice 3/8" (9mm) over straps at DOTS (see pattern), being careful not to twist straps. Sew in place.

7. Apply fastener; see FINISHING BACK OPENING EDGES, page 9, Steps 1-6. ♥

FRILLED SKIRT

1. With RIGHT sides together, stitch SKIRT FRONT to SKIRT BACK at side seams.

2. Press under 1/4" (6mm) on upper edge of skirt. Sew 1/8" (3mm) from pressed edge.

3. Press under 1/4" (6mm) on lower edge of RUFFLE. Sew 1/8" (3mm) from pressed edge.

4. To gather upper edge of ruffle, machine-baste 1/4" and 1/8" (6mm and 3mm) from raw edge.

5. With RIGHT sides together, pin ruffle to lower edge of skirt, matching centers and having edges even. Pull up bobbin threads and adjust gathers to fit. Stitch in place. Press seam allowance toward skirt. On OUTSIDE, topstitch skirt 1/8" (3mm) from ruffle seam.

6. With RIGHT sides together, sew up center back, **1/2" (1.2cm)** from edge, stitching from hem to DOT (see pattern).

7. Apply fastener; see FINISHING BACK OPENING EDGES, page 9. ♥

POWER SUIT

Felt makes easy work of the Power Suit. It doesn't ravel, so you can leave the edges unfinished. Also, it doesn't have grain, so you can place the pattern pieces any direction to fit them on pre-cut felt pieces.

This outfit is designed to make an impression, especially in colors such as hot pink, emerald green or electric blue. The jacket's asymmetric hem brings individuality to a traditional silhouette.

*Be sure to use **polyester felt**, not wool, due to the way wool shrinks when pressed. In garments of this size, the shrinkage is enough to make them too small to fit the doll.*

SUPPLIES

9"x12" pre-cut polyester felt fabric, 2 pieces
3/4" (19mm) wide Velcro® Sleek & Thin™ sew-on tape
Paper clip or 18 gauge craft wire; wire cutters & file
1/2" (1cm) diameter marking pen

Note: PATTERN IS ON PAGES 77-81. Pattern includes seam allowances. Seam allowances are 1/4" (6mm) unless instructions indicate otherwise.

JACKET

From Felt only.

1. Stitch RIGHT JACKET and LEFT JACKET together along center back seam.

2. Stitch entire seam of sleeves and sides, pivoting needle at armpit. Clip seam allowance at armpits. Trim seam allowance of sleeves to 1/8" (3mm).

3. With COLLAR against INSIDE of jacket, pin neck edges together, matching DOTS (see pattern), edges even and center backs aligned. Sew in place along edge by hand with whipstitch.

4. For BUCKLE, wrap wire once around marking pen to make a ring (X). Slide ring off marker and bend tail of wire across center to make a bar (Y). Trim away excess with wire cutters (Z). Smooth cuts with a file.

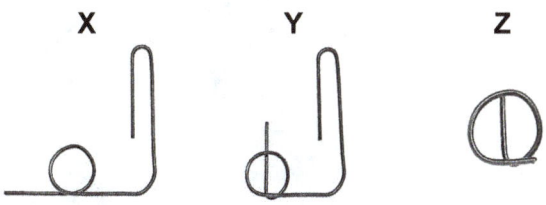

Thread BELT over center bar of buckle; turn end under 1" (2.5cm) and sew in place.

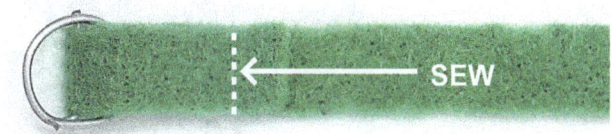

Try jacket & belt on doll and trim belt to desired length. ♥

PANTS

From Felt only.

1. Stitch center front seam from upper edge to DOT (see pattern). Clip curves.

2. Stitch side seams by sewing Side A to Side B (see pattern). Press seam open.

Tip: Roll a piece of paper or cardstock tightly and insert in pant leg to make a *seam roll* for pressing.

3. To topstitch waistline, sew 1/8" (3mm) from edge.

4. Apply fastener; see FINISHING BACK OPENING EDGES, page 9. ♥

T-SHIRT DRESS

Simple lines make this dress speedy to sew. The neckline is straight, and there is no back opening on the pullover style.

Pictured with Inspiration Necklace, page 49.

SUPPLIES

T-shirt or jersey knit fabric, 1/4 yd (.23m)

Note: PATTERN IS ON PAGE 83. Pattern includes seam allowances. Seam allowances are 1/4" (6mm) unless instructions indicate otherwise.

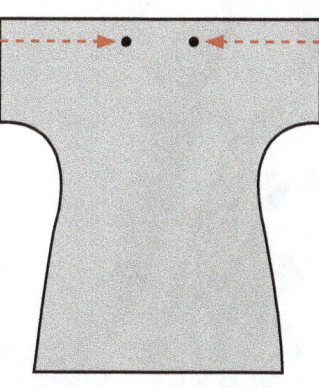

1. With RIGHT sides together, stitch fronts to backs at shoulder seams from end of sleeve to DOT (see pattern), leaving an opening between dots.

2. Press entire seam open, pressing under 1/4" (6mm) between dots to create neck opening.

3. On OUTSIDE, topstitch 1/8" (3mm) on each side of shoulder seam, including pressed edges of neckline (see red stitchlines below).

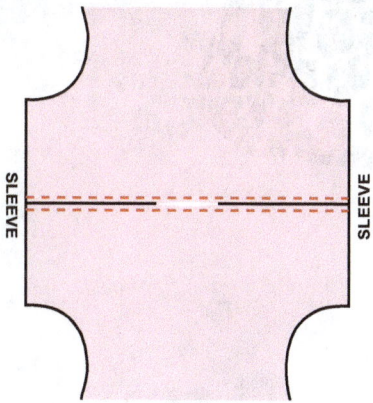

4. Press under 1/4" on sleeve ends. Sew 1/8" (3mm) from pressed edge.

5. Press under 1/4" (6mm) on lower edges of garment. Sew 1/8" (3mm) from pressed edge.

6. With RIGHT sides together, stitch entire seam of underarms and sides. ♥

FINGERLESS GLOVES & FOOTLESS STOCKINGS

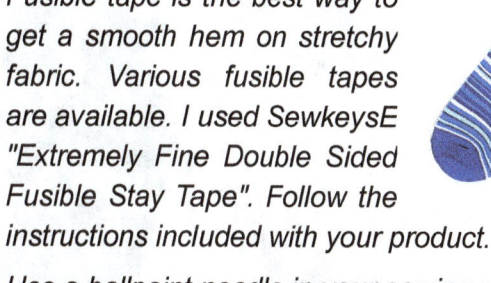

These accessories are made from socks or stretch knit fabric. The mini-stripe socks used here were purchased on Amazon.

Fusible tape is the best way to get a smooth hem on stretchy fabric. Various fusible tapes are available. I used SewkeysE "Extremely Fine Double Sided Fusible Stay Tape". Follow the instructions included with your product.

Use a ballpoint needle in your sewing machine.

SUPPLIES

Adult crew sock or stretch knit fabric

Double-sided fusible tape, 1/4" (6mm) wide

Note: PATTERNS ARE ON PAGE 83. Pattern includes seam allowances. Seam allowances are 1/4" (6mm) unless instructions indicate otherwise.

1. On each GLOVE or STOCKING, press fusible tape to WRONG side along upper & lower edge. Peel away protective paper backing from tape.

2. Press under 1/4" (6mm) on upper and lower edge of each glove or stocking. Sew over raw edge using a zigag stitch so raw edge is encased.

3. With RIGHT sides together, fold garment lengthwise so that edges meet. Stitch seam. Trim seam allowance to 1/8" (3mm). ♥

Tip: *To make dressing your doll in the Fingerless Gloves easier, slip small plastic covers over the doll's hands. These can be made by cutting triangles from the corners of a sandwich bag.*

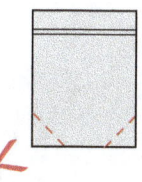

RUFFLE-TRIM BLOUSE

SUPPLIES

Lightweight woven or knit cotton fabric, 1/8 yd (.11m)

3/4" (19mm) wide Velcro® Sleek & Thin™ sew-on tape

1" (2.5cm) wide ribbon: organza, grosgrain or satin

3 beads, 4mm

All-purpose glue stick, optional

Note: PATTERN IS ON PAGE 83. Pattern includes seam allowances. Seam allowances are 1/4" (6mm) unless instructions indicate otherwise.

1. To make darts, fold on solid line, RIGHT SIDES TOGETHER. Sew on dotted line. Press fold of darts toward back.

2. On armholes, machine stitch 1/4" (6mm) from edge. Press or glue* under on stitchline, clipping curves. Sew 1/8" (3mm) from turned edge.
* Note: To glue, lightly dab glue stick along wrong side of seam allowance and finger-press in place.

3. With RIGHT sides together, stitch front to back at shoulder seams.

4. On neckline, stitch 1/4" (6mm) from edge. Press or glue under on stitchline, clipping curves. Sew 1/8" (3mm) from turned edge.

5. Press under 1/4" (6mm) on lower edge of blouse. Sew 1/8" from pressed edge.

6. Apply fasteners; see FINISHING BACK OPENING EDGES, page 9, Steps 1-6.

7. For RUFFLE, cut a 5" length of ribbon. To gather, machine baste 3/8" (8mm) from each long edge.

8. At one end of ruffle, knot all thread tails together. At other end, pull up bobbin threads and adjust gathers until ruffle measures 2" (5cm) long as pictured in Fig. A.

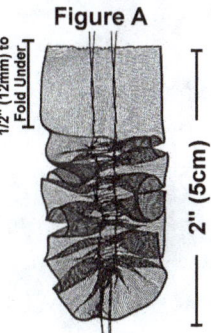

Figure A
1/2" (12mm) to Fold Under
2" (5cm)

9. Pin ruffle to center front of blouse, turning 1/2" (1cm) over neckline to inside of blouse. Hand sew ruffle in place. Sew beads to ruffle. ♥

FULL SKIRT

SUPPLIES

Lightweight woven cotton fabric, 1/4 yd (.23m)

1 snap

Note: PATTERN IS ON PAGE 85. Pattern includes seam allowances. Seam allowances are 1/4" (6mm) unless instructions indicate otherwise.

1. To gather SKIRT, machine baste 1/4" and 1/8" (6mm and 3mm) from one long edge. This will be the waistline.

2. Press under 1/4" (6mm) on lower edge of skirt. Sew 1/8" from pressed edge.

3. Fold WAISTBAND in half lengthwise, WRONG sides together. Press.

4. Pin raw edge of waistband to gathered edge of skirt, RIGHT sides together, matching centers and having edges even. Pull up bobbin threads and adjust gathers to fit. Stitch.

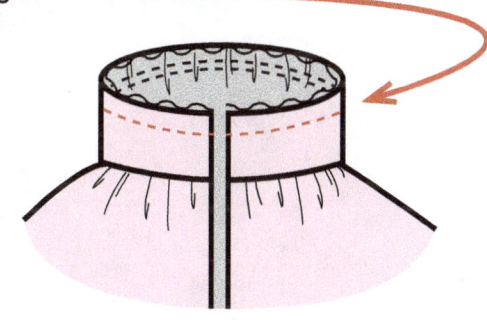

Press seam allowance toward skirt, clipping seam allowance of **waistband** at 1/2" (1.2cm) intervals.

5. With RIGHT sides together, sew up center back of skirt, **1/2" (1.2cm)** from edge, stitching from hem to DOT (see pattern). Press seam allowance to one side.

6. Turn under 1/2" (1.2cm) on one back opening edge. Sew prong half of snap to INSIDE on waistband. Sew socket half of snap to OUTSIDE on opposite edge. ♥

27

SCRUBS

SUPPLIES

Lightweight woven cotton fabric, 1/4 yd (.23m)

1/4" (6mm) wide braided elastic

Elastic cord (for mask)

Single-Fold Bias Tape, 1/2" (12.7mm) wide

3/4" (19mm) wide Velcro® Sleek & Thin™ sew-on tape

Note: PATTERNS ARE ON PAGE 87. Pattern includes seam allowances. Seam allowances are 1/4" (6mm) unless instructions indicate otherwise.

SHIRT

1. On neckline, sew 1/4" (6mm) from edge with a short stitch length, pivoting at center front. Clip seam allowance at center front and clip curves.

2. Using stitchline as a guide, press under 1/4" (6mm) on neck edge. Sew 1/8" (3mm) from pressed edge.

3. Press under 1/4" (6mm) on edge of armholes. Sew 1/8" (3mm) from pressed edge.

4. With RIGHT sides together, stitch side seams. Clip underarm curves.

5. Press under 1/4" (6mm) on lower edge of shirt. Sew 1/8" (3mm) from pressed edge.

6. Press under 1/4" (6mm) on upper edge of POCKETS. Sew 1/8" (3mm) from pressed edge. Press under 1/4" (6mm) on remaining edges.

7. Pin pockets to shirt as indicated by pocket lines on pattern. Sew in place along side & lower edges.

8. Apply fastener; see FINISHING BACK OPENING EDGES, page 9, Steps 1-6. ♥

PANTS

1. For casing, press under 1/2" (1.3cm) on upper edge. Sew 3/8" (9mm) from pressed edge.

2. Cut elastic 4" (10cm) long. Using a small safety pin, insert elastic thru casing & sew securely at ends.

3. Press under 1/4" (6mm) on lower edges of pants. Sew 1/8" from pressed edges.

4. With RIGHT sides together, stitch center back seam.

5. With RIGHT sides together, stitch front to back at inside leg edges. Clip seam allowance on each side of crotch. ♥

CAP

1. Cut an 18" (45cm) piece of bias tape. Open one side of tape and align its raw edge with edge of CAP, RIGHT sides together. Sew along crease of bias tape, about 1/4" (6mm) from edge, until you overlap the starting point. Cut off excess tape.

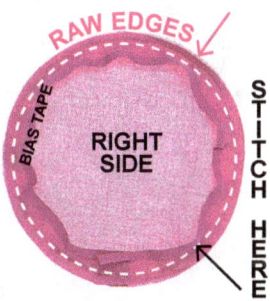

2. Fold tape over edge of fabric to WRONG side, creating a casing. Press casing flat.

3. Sew close to inner folded edge of tape, leaving a 1/2" (1.3cm) opening for the elastic to be inserted.

4. Cut elastic 5 1/4" (13.25cm) long. Using a small safety pin, insert elastic thru casing, gathering the fabric as you work the elastic thru. Overlap ends of elastic 1/4" (6mm) & sew them together securely.

5. Push elastic completely into casing and sew opening in bias tape closed. ♥

FACE MASK

1. Press under 1/4" (6mm) on *long* edges. Sew 1/8" (3mm) from pressed edges.

2. For casings, press under 1/2" (1.2cm) on *short* edges. Sew 1/4" (6mm) from pressed edges.

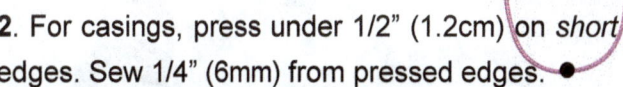

3. Cut elastic cord 9" (20cm) long. Insert elastic thru casings and tie ends together securely with an overhand knot. Hide knot inside a casing. Bring DOTS together (see photo) to place on doll. ♥

CARGO CAPRI PANTS

The pockets can be omitted for a different look.

SUPPLIES

Lightweight woven cotton fabric, 1/4 yd (.23m)
1/8" (6mm) wide braided elastic
2 buttons, 1/4" (6mm) diameter

Note: PATTERN IS ON PAGE 89. Pattern includes seam allowances. Seam allowances are 1/4" (6mm) unless instructions indicate otherwise.

1. Prepare each POCKET as follows: Turn upper edge of pocket to OUTSIDE along foldline (see pattern). Stitch 1/4" (6mm) along sides & lower edges.

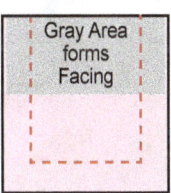

2. Turn facing to INSIDE, turning under sides & lower edges 1/4" (6mm). Press. On OUTSIDE, topstitch close to sides & upper edges of pocket between DOTS (see pattern).

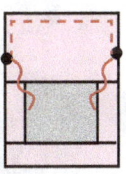

3. On OUTSIDE, pin pocket to pants along pocket lines (see pattern). Topstitch close to side & lower edges between DOTS.

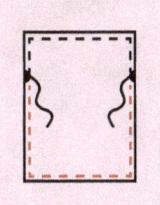

4. Turn flap down 3/8" (9mm). Press. Sew button to flap & pocket as pictured.

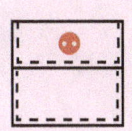

5. Stitch center front seam of PANTS FRONT & BACK with RIGHT sides together. Clip curve.

6. For waistline casing, press under 5/8" (15mm) on upper edge. Sew 3/8" (9mm) from pressed edge.

7. Cut elastic 3" (7.5cm) long. Using a small safety pin, insert elastic thru casing having ends even. Sew securely across ends.

8. Press under 1/4" (6mm) on lower edges of pants. Sew 1/8" from pressed edges.

9. With RIGHT sides together, stitch center back seam. Clip curve.

10. With RIGHT sides together, stitch front to back at inner leg edges, matching crotch seams. Clip seam allowance on each side of crotch. ♥

SHORT-SLEEVE TOP

SUPPLIES

Lightweight knit or woven cotton fabric, 1/8 yd (.11m)
3/4" (19mm) wide Velcro® Sleek & Thin™ sew-on tape
All purpose glue stick, optional

Note: PATTERN IS ON PAGE 89. Pattern includes seam allowances. Seam allowances are 1/4" (6mm) unless instructions indicate otherwise.

1. With RIGHT sides together, stitch fronts to backs at shoulder seams.

2. On neckline, stitch 1/4" (6mm) from edge. Press or glue* under on stitchline, clipping curves. Sew 1/8" (3mm) from turned edge.
* Note: To glue, lightly dab glue stick along wrong side of seam allowance and finger-press in place.

3. Press under 1/4" on sleeve edges. Sew 1/8" (3mm) from pressed edge.

4. With RIGHT sides together, stitch entire seam of underarms and sides, pivoting at armpit. Clip seam allowance at armpit.

5. Press under 1/4" (6mm) on lower edge of shirt. Sew 1/8" (3mm) from pressed edge.

6. Apply fastener; see FINISHING BACK OPENING EDGES, page 9, Steps 1-6. ♥

V-NECK DAY DRESS

The Day Dress is a style well-suited for delicate floral prints. The dress is also cute with a ribbon tied around the waist.

SUPPLIES

Lightweight woven cotton fabric, 1/8 yd (.11m)
3/4" (19mm) wide Velcro® Sleek & Thin™ sew-on tape

Note: PATTERN IS ON PAGE 91. Pattern includes seam allowances. Seam allowances are 1/4" (6mm) unless instructions indicate otherwise.

1. Sew darts on BODICE FRONT and BODICE BACK. Press darts toward center.

2. With RIGHT sides together, stitch bodice front to bodice back at shoulders.

3. On neckline, sew 1/4" (6mm) from edge with a short stitch length, pivoting at center front. Clip seam allowance at center front and clip curves.

4. Using stitchline as a guide, press under 1/4" (6mm) on neck edge. Sew 1/8" (3mm) from pressed edge.

5. Make clips in side seams at DOTS (see pattern). Press under 1/4" (6mm) between dots to create armholes. Sew 1/8" from pressed edge.

6. With RIGHT sides together, stitch bodice front to bodice back at side seams.

7. Press under 1/4" (6mm) on lower edge of SKIRT. Sew 1/8" (3mm) from pressed edge.

8. To gather upper edge of skirt, machine baste 1/4" and 1/8" (6mm and 3mm) from raw edge.

9. With RIGHT sides together, pin skirt to bodice at waistline seam, matching centers and having back edges even. Pull up bobbin threads and adjust gathers to fit. Stitch in place. Press seam allowance toward bodice.

10. On OUTSIDE, topstitch bodice 1/8" (3mm) from waistline seam.

11. With RIGHT sides together, sew up center back of skirt, **1/2" (1.2cm)** from edge, stitching from hem to DOT (see pattern).

12. Apply fastener; see FINISHING BACK OPENING EDGES, page 9. ♥

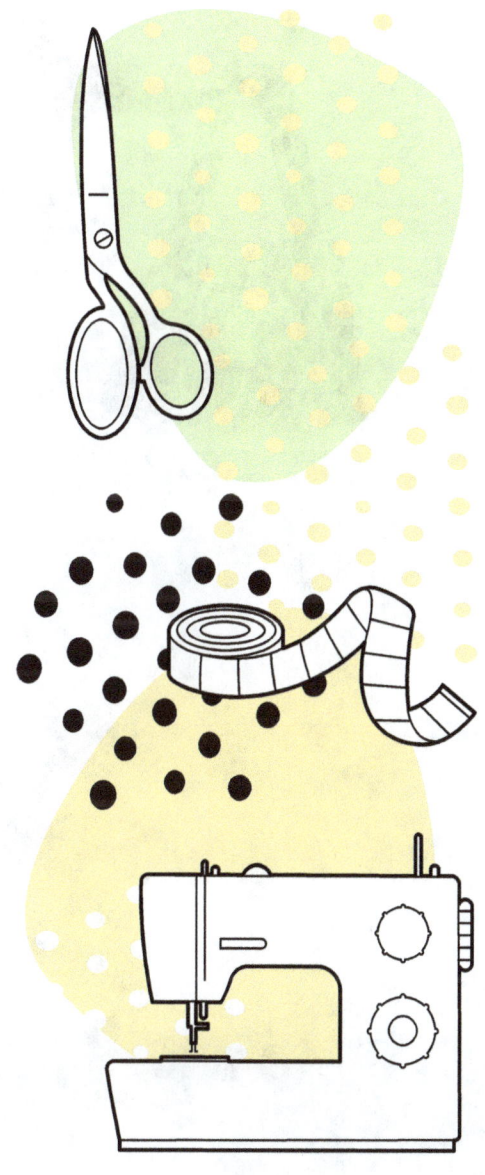

SHELL

The Shell is pictured with Ruched Purse, page 62.

SUPPLIES

Lightweight woven or knit cotton fabric, 1/4 yd (.23m)
3/4" (19mm) wide Velcro® Sleek & Thin™ sew-on tape
All-purpose glue stick, optional

Note: PATTERN IS ON PAGE 93. Pattern includes seam allowances. Seam allowances are 1/4" (6mm) unless instructions indicate otherwise.

1. On neckline, stitch 1/4" (6mm) from edge. Press or glue* under on stitchline, clipping curves. Sew 1/8" (3mm) from turned edge.
* Note: To glue, lightly dab glue stick along wrong side of seam allowance and finger-press in place.

2. On armholes, machine stitch 1/4" (6mm) from edge. Press or glue under on stitchline, clipping curves. Sew 1/8" (3mm) from turned edge.

3. With RIGHT sides together, stitch front to back at underarm seams. Clip curves.

4. Press under 1/4" (6mm) on lower edge of shell. Sew 1/8" from pressed edge.

5. Apply fastener; see FINISHING BACK OPENING EDGES, page 9, Steps 1-6. ♥

INFINITY SCARF

SUPPLIES

Cotton, silk, chiffon or lightweight jersey fabric

Note: PATTERN IS ON PAGE 123.

1. Press under 1/4" (6mm) on one short end.

2. With RIGHT sides together, fold scarf so that long edges meet. Sew together 1/4" from edge.

3. Using a small safety pin or loop turner (see page 7), turn right side out. Do not press.

4. With tweezers, tuck raw end inside pressed end and hand-sew together with whip stitch. ♥

PENCIL PANTS

Leather-look pants are glamorous and edgy! For this pattern, the faux leather must be thin and stretchy in order to turn the pants right-side out. You can find this fabric on Amazon or Etsy. Be sure to use a stretch needle in your sewing machine. You likely won't be able to press your leatherette (try a test); so turn the hems under and hold them in place with your fingers as you sew.

SUPPLIES

Lightweight poly-spandex stretch leatherette, woven cotton or denim fabric, 1/4 yd (.23m)
1 snap

Note: PATTERN IS ON PAGE 93. Pattern includes seam allowances. Seam allowances are 1/4" (6mm) unless instructions indicate otherwise.

1. Sew darts on back sections. Turn darts toward center.

2. With RIGHT sides together, sew fronts to backs at sides.

3. With RIGHT sides together, stitch center front seam of pants front sections. Clip curves.

4. To staystitch waistline, sew 1/4" (6mm) from edge. Clip to stitching. Turn under on stitchline and sew 1/8" (3mm) from turned edge.

5. Turn under 1/4" (6mm) hem on bottom of pant legs. Sew 1/8" from turned edges.

6. With RIGHT sides together, sew center back seam of pants back sections BETWEEN DOTS with **1/2" (1.2cm)** seam allowance, leaving an opening above dots. Trim seam allowance to 1/4" between dots. Clip curves.

7. With RIGHT sides together, stitch fronts to backs at inner leg edges matching crotch seams. Clip seam allowance on each side of crotch.

8. Turn under 1/2" (1.2cm) on one back opening edge. Sew prong half of snap to INSIDE of this edge. Sew socket half of snap to OUTSIDE of opposite edge. ♥

HOODED CAPE

The cape is made from polyester fleece, also known as polar fleece. Ornamental overcasting adorns the edges of the cape pictured. Other options include zigzag, blanket stitching by hand or simply leaving the edges raw since fleece won't fray or ravel.

The Right Side of fleece can be difficult to distinguish. It is generally smoother and less fuzzy compared to the Wrong Side.

Pictured with Pencil Pants, pattern on page 35.

SUPPLIES

Medium-weight polyester fleece, 1/3 yd (.30m)
1 hook & eye

Note: PATTERN IS ON PAGE 95. Pattern includes seam allowances. Seam allowances are 1/4" (6mm) unless instructions indicate otherwise.

1. On CAPE, cut **center front** open along foldline.

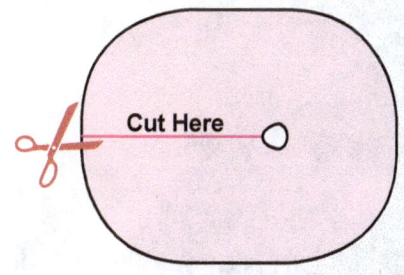

2. Fold HOOD at center back, RIGHT SIDES TOGETHER and stitch top seam along seam line indicated on pattern. Trim seam allowance to 1/8" (3mm).

3. With RIGHT SIDES TOGETHER, pin neck edge of hood to cape, matching front edges and center backs. Stitch.

4. Press seam toward cape. On OUTSIDE, topstitch cape close to neckline seam.

5. For optional embellishment around edges of cape and hood, overcast or zigzag by machine, or blanket stitch by hand.

6. Sew hook & eye at neckline. ♥

37

HI-LO COAT

Polyester fleece is used here. This fabric won't fray or ravel, so the edges can be left unhemmed. The ribbon belt has a buckle at center front and a snap at the back.

SUPPLIES

Medium-weight polyester fleece, 1/4 yd (.23m)

8 craft gems, 1/4" (6mm)

3/16" (5mm) Glue Dots or Gem-Tac or Jewel-It glue

Satin ribbon, 3/8" (8mm) wide

Paper clip or 18 gauge craft wire; wire cutters & file

1/2" (1cm) diameter marking pen

1 hook & eye

1 snap

Glitter nail polish, optional

Note: PATTERN IS ON PAGE 97. Pattern includes seam allowances. Seam allowances are 1/4" (6mm) unless instructions indicate otherwise.

1. With RIGHT sides together, stitch BODICE FRONTS to BODICE BACK at shoulders. Trim seam allowance to 1/8" (3mm).

2. With RIGHT sides together, stitch entire seam of underarms and sides. Clip seam allowance at armpit. Trim seam allowance to 1/8" (3mm).

3. Pin PEPLUM to bodice, RIGHT sides together, matching center-backs and having front edges even. Stitch in place. Press seam allowance toward bodice. On OUTSIDE, topstitch bodice close to waistline seam.

4. Fold lapels on creaselines and tack in place with a hand stitch at each DOT (see pattern). Glue gems to lapels at each DOT.

5. Sew hook & eye to INSIDE at waistline.

6. For BUCKLE, wrap wire once around marking pen to make a ring (X). Slide ring off marker and bend tail of wire across center to make a bar (Y). Trim away excess with wire cutters (Z). Smooth cuts with a file. Paint with glitter nail polish, if desired.

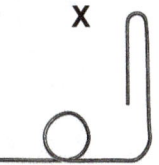  

7. For BELT, cut ribbon 6" (15cm) long. Press ends under 1/2" (1cm). Sew in place or secure with a dab of glue stick. Thread belt thru buckle, positioning buckle at center. Sew snap to ends of belt. ♥

COLUMN GOWN

See page 6 for tips for working with sequin fabric.

To hem the upper and lower edges of the dress, turn the fabric under 1/4" and hold in place with your fingers as you sew. Use a stretch needle in your sewing machine.

SUPPLIES

Sequin or stretch knit fabric, 1/4 yd (.23m)

Ribbon, 1/8" (3mm) wide

Note: PATTERN IS ON PAGE 99. Pattern includes seam allowances. Seam allowances are 1/4" (6mm) unless instructions indicate otherwise.

1. Turn under 1/4" (6mm) on upper edge of FRONT and BACK. Zigzag in place.

2. Turn under 1/4" (6mm) on lower edge of front and back. Zigzag in place.

3. With RIGHT sides together, stitch side seams with zigzag.

4. Cut 2 pieces of ribbon for shoulder straps, each 2 1/2" (6cm) long. Lap upper edge of dress 1/2" (1cm) over straps at DOTS (see pattern), being careful not to twist straps. Sew straps in place. ♥

FRINGE DRESS

The Fringe Dress gets its fitted, feminine shape from double-pointed darts. To see video demos of this type of dart, search "sewing a double-pointed dart" at YouTube.com.

T-Shirt fabric works well for this pattern. Many craft stores sell inexpensive T-Shirts which are ideal.

Pictured with Friendship Bracelets, page 49.

Tips:

- For perfect fringe, place 2 strips of Scotch Double-Sided Removable Tape on back side of pattern, behind the red slash lines, before pinning pattern to fabric. This will prevent the fabric from shifting when you cut your fringe.

- After cutting out the dress, transfer the markings for the double-sided darts to the fabric as follows: Start by poking holes in <u>pattern only</u> at all 4 points of the dart. This can be done with a toothpick or a thin skewer. Then, with the pattern in position on WRONG side of fabric, take a disappearing ink marking pen, or chalk pencil, and make dots thru holes in pattern onto fabric. Remove pattern and connect dots with a ruler.

SUPPLIES

Lightweight jersey knit fabric, 1/4 yd (.23m)

1 snap

Scotch Double-Sided Removable Tape

All purpose glue stick, optional

Note: PATTERN IS ON PAGE 101. Pattern includes seam allowances. Seam allowances are 1/4" (6mm) unless instructions indicate otherwise.

1. Cut fringe as shown with red lines on pattern.

2. To make darts in DRESS, fold on solid line, RIGHT SIDES TOGETHER. Sew on dotted line. Press fold of darts toward back.

3. On armholes, stitch 1/4" (6mm) from edge. Press or glue* under on stitchline, clipping curves. Sew 1/8" (3mm) from turned edge.
* Note: To glue, lightly dab glue stick along wrong side of seam allowance and finger-press in place.

4. With RIGHT sides together, stitch front to back at shoulder seams.

5. On neckline, stitch 1/4" (6mm) from edge. Press or glue under on stitchline, clipping curves. Sew 1/8" (3mm) from turned edge.

6. With RIGHT sides together, sew center back seam **1/2" (1.2cm)** from edge, between DOTS (see pattern).

7. Turn under 1/2" (1.2cm) on one back opening edge. Sew prong half of snap to INSIDE of this edge. Sew socket half of snap to OUTSIDE on opposite edge. ♥

TENT DRESS

Cut-on sleeves and simple lines make this dress a good starter project for beginning sewists.

SUPPLIES

Lightweight woven or knit cotton fabric, 1/4 yd (.23m)

3/4" (19mm) wide Velcro® Sleek & Thin™ sew-on tape

All purpose glue stick, optional

Note: PATTERN IS ON PAGE 103. Pattern includes seam allowances. Seam allowances are 1/4" (6mm) unless instructions indicate otherwise.

1. With RIGHT sides together, stitch FRONT to BACK at shoulders.

2. Press under 1/4" (6mm) on end of sleeves. Sew 1/8" (3mm) from pressed edge.

3. On neckline, stitch 1/4" (6mm) from edge. Press or glue* under on stitchline, clipping curves. Sew 1/8" (3mm) from turned edge.
* Note: To glue, lightly dab glue stick along wrong side of seam allowance and finger-press in place.

4. With RIGHT sides together, stitch entire seam of underarms and sides. Clip underarm curves.

5. Press under 1/4" (6mm) on lower edge of dress. Sew 1/8" (3mm) from pressed edge.

6. With RIGHT sides together, sew up center back of dress, **1/2" (1.2cm)** from edge, stitching from hem to DOT (see pattern).

7. Apply fastener; see FINISHING BACK OPENING EDGES, page 9. ♥

BUCKET BAG

A colorful purse adds pizzazz to any outfit! This one is easy to make — and big enough to hold a few doll-size accessories.

SUPPLIES

9"x12" pre-cut felt fabric, 1 piece

5 beads

Fabric glue

Note: PATTERN IS ON PAGE 103. Pattern includes seam allowances. Seam allowances are 1/4" (6mm).

1. With RIGHT sides together, crease bag on foldline and stitch side seams.

2. On INSIDE, to form flat bottom for bag, finger-press side seams open, then fold bottom ends as shown in Fig. A. Stitch 1/2" (1.2cm) from tips, thru all layers, as shown by red dotted line below. Trim seam allowance to 1/4" (6mm). Turn bag right-side out.

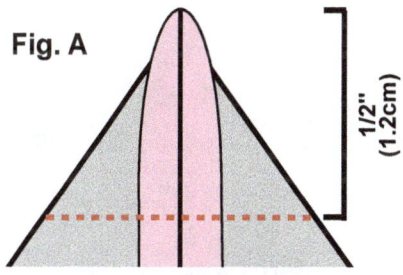

Fig. A — 1/2" (1.2cm)

3. For closure, cut a small slit in flap (see pattern). Sew bead to purse under slit.

4. Lap ends of handles 1/2" (1.2cm) over upper edge of bag at DOTS (see pattern), being careful not to twist handles. Glue in place. Sew beads to ends of handles as pictured. ♥

TURTLENECK SHIRT & STRAIGHT SKIRT

I used thin cotton knit fabric — repurposed from a baby garment — to make the outfit pictured. The cutting was planned to have a floral motif centered on the front of the shirt.

You can easily give this outfit a different look by changing the length of the skirt. For an elegant ensemble, it would be stunning made from black fabric and worn with a necklace of pearl beads!

SUPPLIES

Lightweight knit or woven fabric, 1/4 yd (.23m)

1/4" (6mm) wide braided elastic

3/4" (19mm) wide Velcro® Sleek & Thin™ sew-on tape

Disappearing ink marking pen or tailor's chalk

Note: PATTERNS ARE ON PAGE 105. Pattern includes seam allowances. Seam allowances are 1/4" (6mm) unless instructions indicate otherwise.

TURTLENECK SHIRT

1. To staystitch, sew 1/4" (6mm) from neck edge on FRONT and BACKS using a short stitch length.

2. With RIGHT sides together, stitch front to back at shoulders.

3. Press under 1/4" (6mm) hem on ends of sleeves. Sew 1/8" (3mm) from pressed edge.

4. CLIP CURVES of neckline to staystitching (see page 8) and press under 1/4" (6mm).

5. With RIGHT sides together, fold COLLAR in half lengthwise. Stitch across ends. Trim seam allowance to 1/8" (3mm). Turn collar; press.

6. Draw a **placement line** 1/4" (6mm) from raw edge of collar with disappearing ink marking pen or tailor's chalk.

7. Pin pressed neck edge of shirt to collar on **placement line**, matching centers. Topstitch in place.

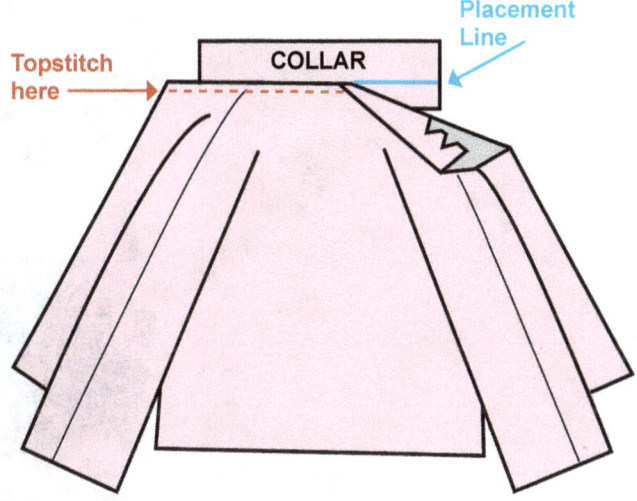

8. With RIGHT sides together, stitch entire seam of underarms & sides. Clip seam allowance at armpit.

9. Press under 1/4" (6mm) hem on lower edge of shirt. Sew 1/8" (3mm) from pressed edge.

10. Apply fastener; see FINISHING BACK OPENING EDGES, page 9, Steps 1-6. ♥

STRAIGHT SKIRT

1. Press under 1/4" (6mm) on lower edge of SKIRT. Sew 1/8" (3mm) from pressed edge.

2. For casing, press under 5/8" (15mm) at upper edge of skirt. Sew 3/8" (1cm) from pressed edge.

3. Cut elastic 3 1/2" (9cm) long. Using a small safety pin, insert elastic thru casing and sew securely at ends.

4. With RIGHT sides together, stitch center back seam. ♥

FRINGE BELT

The free-spirited Fringe Belt can made be from felt, faux-leather or suede. Pair it with shorts, pants, skirts or dresses to give any outfit a festival vibe! Pictured with Friendship Bracelets, page 49.

SUPPLIES

Felt, Faux-Leather or Suede, 9"x12" piece
Paper clip or 18 gauge craft wire; wire cutters & file
1/2" (1cm) diameter marking pen
7 metal beads, 3mm
Scotch Double-Sided Removable Tape

Note: PATTERN IS ON PAGE 107.

Cutting Tips:

- For perfect fringe, place 3 strips of Scotch Double-Sided Removable Tape on back side of pattern, behind the red slash lines, before pinning or clipping pattern to material (see Fig. A). This will prevent the material from shifting when you cut your fringe.

Figure A

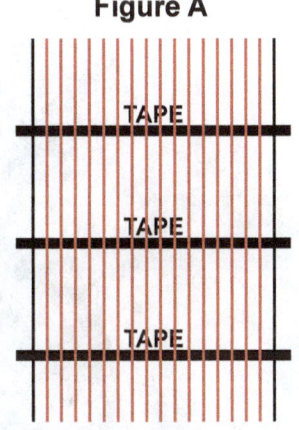

- To place pattern on Faux-Leather or Suede, use Mini Fabric Clips instead of pins to avoid puncturing the material.

1. Cut fringe as shown with red lines on pattern.
2. For BUCKLE, wrap wire once around marking pen to make a ring (X). Slide ring off marker and bend tail of wire across center to make a bar (Y). Trim away excess with wire cutters (Z). Smooth cuts with a file.

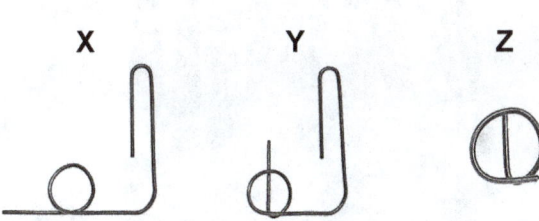

3. Thread short end of BELT over center bar of buckle; turn end under 1" (2.5cm) and sew in place.

4. Sew beads to belt as indicated by DOTS on pattern. ♥

BRA TOP

This pattern is designed for stable, woven fabric. To make it from a stretch knit, back the fabric with light-weight fusible interfacing.

SUPPLIES

Lightweight woven cotton fabric, 1/8 yd (.11m)
Faux-leather or 1/8" (3mm) wide ribbon
3/4" (19mm) wide Velcro® Sleek & Thin™ sew-on tape

Note: PATTERN IS ON PAGE 107.

1. Sew darts in BRA. Press toward center.

2. Press under 1/4" (6mm) on upper and lower edges of bra. Sew 1/8" (3mm) from pressed edges.

3. For each strap, cut faux leather 1/8" x 2.5" (3 x 63mm) or use 1/8" wide (3mm) ribbon. Lap upper edge of bra 3/8" (8mm) over straps at DOTS (see pattern), being careful not to twist straps. Sew in place.

4. Apply fastener; see FINISHING BACK OPENING EDGES, page 9, Steps 1-6. ♥

JEANS SHORTS

The shorts pictured were made from well-worn denim harvested from thrift-store toddler jeans. The topstitching can be done with matching or contrasting thread.

SUPPLIES

Lightweight denim, 1/8 yd (.11m)
Disappearing ink marking pen or chalk pencil
1 snap

Note: PATTERN IS ON PAGE 107. Pattern includes seam allowances. Seam allowances are 1/4" (6mm) unless instructions indicate otherwise.

1. Clip for fringe as shown with red lines on pattern.

2. Sew darts on back sections. Press darts toward center.

3. For mock fly, topstitch <u>one</u> shorts FRONT as shown on patttern with dashed lines. For mock pockets, topstitch <u>both</u> shorts fronts as shown on pattern with dashed lines. *Templates are provided that you can position to draw stitchlines with a disappearing ink marking pen or chalk pencil.*

4. With RIGHT sides together, sew fronts to backs at sides. Press seam toward back.

5. On OUTSIDE, topstitch backs along side seams, sewing 1/8" (3mm) from seam.

6. With RIGHT sides together, stitch center front seam of shorts front sections. Clip curve.

7. To staystitch waistline, sew 1/4" (6mm) from edge. Press under 1/4" (6mm) using stitchline for a guide. Topstitch 1/8" (3mm) from pressed edge.

8. With RIGHT sides together, sew center back seam of shorts back sections BETWEEN DOTS with **1/2" (1.2cm)** seam allowance, leaving an opening above dots. Trim seam allowance to 1/4" between dots. Clip curves.

9. With RIGHT sides together, stitch fronts to backs at inner leg edges, matching crotch seams. Clip seam allowance on each side of crotch.

10. Press under 1/2" (1.2cm) on one back opening edge. Sew prong half of snap to INSIDE of this edge. Sew socket half of snap to OUTSIDE of opposite edge.

11. To fray the hem, take a sewing pin and gently pick at the horizontal white threads at the edge of each clip. The threads will loosen, giving a frayed effect. ♥

FRIENDSHIP BRACELET

You can thread beads on the cord by hand or with a beading needle.

Need help with your knot? YouTube.com has a lot of video demos for knotting elastic bracelets.

SUPPLIES

Seed beads, 8/0

Stretch Magic clear elastic bead cord, .5mm

Collapsible Eye beading needle, optional

G&S G-S Hypo Cement, optional

1. Pull a length of elastic cord from spool; thread beads on cord until they measure 1" (2.5cm).

2. Cut cord from spool 8" long. Pre-stretch cord by gently pulling a few times.

3. Cross the cord ends and wrap one end thru the loop TWICE before pulling it snug.

4. Gently pull both ends until knot is firm and beads sit close together.

5. Tie a second knot on top of first knot in same manner. Trim ends leaving a bit of allowance. Reinforce knot with a dot of glue, if desired.

INSPIRATION NECKLACE

Combine seed beads and alphabet beads with words of positive affirmation, your doll's name, initials or an XO! Inspirational words include Love, Peace, Joy, Power, Kind, Calm, Hope, Happy, Smile, Brave, Strong, Dream & Trust.

SUPPLIES

Letter beads, 4x7mm

Seed beads, 8/0

Stretch Magic clear elastic bead cord, .5mm

G&S G-S Hypo Cement, optional

1. Pull a length of elastic cord from spool; thread beads on cord until they measure 5" (13cm) or desired length.

2. Cut cord from spool leaving ample excess for tying. Pre-stretch cord by gently pulling a few times.

3. Cross the cord ends and wrap one end thru the loop TWICE before pulling it snug.

4. Gently pull both ends until knot is firm and beads sit close together.

5. Tie a second knot on top of first knot in same manner. Trim ends leaving a bit of allowance. Reinforce knot with a dot of glue, if desired.

BOW MAXI DRESS

For this empire style, an elastic waistline sits just below the bust. The back is fastened with a ribbon bow. Fabric was repurposed from a rayon blouse to make the dress pictured.

SUPPLIES

Lightweight cotton or rayon fabric, 1/4 yd (.23m)

1/4" (6mm) wide braided elastic

1/8" (3mm) wide satin ribbon

Note: PATTERN IS ON PAGES 109-111. Pattern includes seam allowances. Seam allowances are 1/4" (6mm) unless instructions indicate otherwise.

1. Press under 5/8" (15mm) on upper edge of DRESS. For casing, stitch 3/8" (9mm) from pressed edge.

2. Cut elastic 4.5" (11cm) long. Using a small safety pin, insert elastic thru casing and tack securely at ends.

3. Press under 1/4" (6mm) on lower edge of dress. Sew 1/8" from pressed edge.

4. With RIGHT sides together, stitch center back seam of dress.

5. With RIGHT sides together, fold BODICE in half lengthwise. Stitch together along outer raw edges leaving a 2" (5cm) gap for turning.

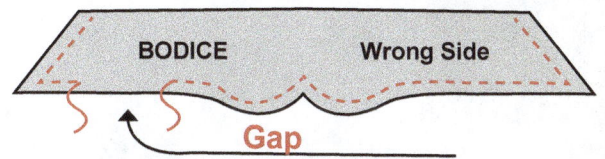

Trim seam allowance to 1/8" (3mm) and TRIM OUTER CORNERS (see page 8).

Turn RIGHT side out. Press. Sew gap closed with slip stitch.

6. Hand-gather along center-front of bodice using a double thread in your needle and running stitch.

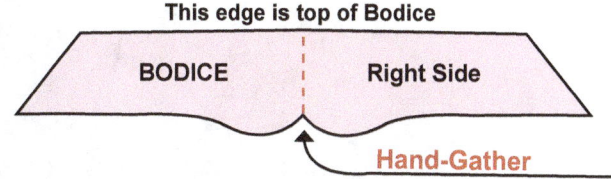

Pull up gathering stitches tight. Knot securely; do not cut thread. Sew center-front of bodice on top of elastic at center-front of dress

7. To embellish bodice, thread a 6" (15cm) piece of ribbon thru a large-eyed hand-sewing needle. Stab thru fabric on stitchline of casing at center front. Pull ribbon thru fabric and remove needle. Tie ends together around **bodice & elastic**, positioning knot and tails inside dress.

8. Cut a 16" (40cm) piece of ribbon. Sew center of ribbon on top of elastic at center-back of dress. ♥

Place the dress on your doll with the elastic just below the bust. Lay the doll face down.

At the back of the dress, criss-cross the ends of the bodice — and tie them together with the ribbon in a bow.

BOAT-NECK TOP & PALAZZO PANTS

See page 6 for tips on working with sequin fabric.

The design of this outfit has very simple lines to facilitate working with sequin fabric: there is no curve to navigate on the neckline and no back opening on the pullover top.

Ironing directly on sequins can melt them. For this reason, you are instructed to "turn under" the hems, rather than pressing them under. Hold the turned edges in place with your fingers as you sew — or use pins or mini sewing clips.

I find it easiest to dress a doll in the Boat-Neck Top by positioning her arms straight up and sliding it down over her arms and head.

SUPPLIES

Sequin or stretch knit fabric, 1/4 yd (.23m)

1/8" (6mm) wide braided elastic

Note: PATTERN IS ON PAGE 113. Pattern includes seam allowances. Seam allowances are 1/4" (6mm) unless instructions indicate otherwise.

BOAT-NECK TOP

1. With RIGHT sides together, stitch fronts to backs at shoulder seams from end of sleeve to DOT (see pattern), leaving an opening between dots.

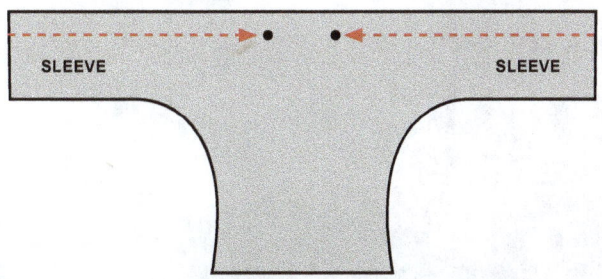

2. Finger-press entire seam open, turning under 1/4" (6mm) between dots to create neck opening.

3. Topstitch 1/8" (3mm) on each side of shoulder seam, (see red stitchlines below). The stitches will catch the neckline seam allowance and finish the neck edge.

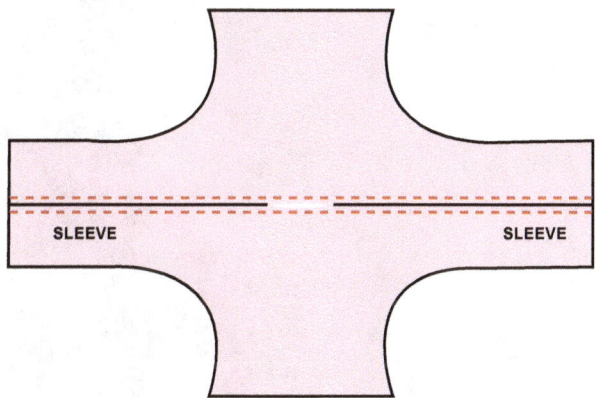

4. Turn under 1/4" on sleeve ends. Sew 1/8" (3mm) from turned edge.

5. Turn under 1/4" (6mm) on lower edges of garment. Sew 1/8" (3mm) from turned edge.

6. With RIGHT sides together, stitch entire seam of underarms and sides. ♥

Tip: *To make dressing easier, slip small plastic covers over the doll's hands. These can be made by cutting triangles from the corners of a sandwich bag.*

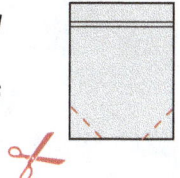

PALAZZO PANTS

1. With RIGHT sides together, stitch center front seam. Clip curve.

2. For casing, turn under 5/8" (15mm) on upper edge. Sew 3/8" (9mm) from turned edge.

3. Cut elastic 3 1/2" (9cm) long. Using a small safety pin, insert elastic thru casing and sew securely at ends.

4. Turn under 1/4" (6mm) on lower edges of pants. Sew 1/8" from turned edges.

5. With RIGHT sides together, stitch center back seam. Clip curve.

6. With RIGHT sides together, stitch front to back at inside leg edges. ♥

PAJAMAS, SLIPPERS & SLEEP MASK

The elastic-waist pajama pants are mid-rise. Check the fit of your elastic before securing it. The slippers can be made 2-tone by using different colors for the soles and straps.

SUPPLIES

Lightweight woven cotton fabric, 1/4 yd (.23m)
Felt, basic or stiffened (slippers & sleep mask)
1/4" wide braided elastic

Note: PATTERNS ARE ON PAGES 115-117. Patterns include seam allowances. Seam allowances are 1/4" (6mm) unless instructions indicate otherwise.

PAJAMA SHIRT

1. With RIGHT sides together, pin neckline of FACING to neckline of SHIRT. Stitch. Clip curves. Turn facing to INSIDE and press in place.

For casing, sew 3/8" (8mm) from pressed edge, leaving a 1/2" (1.3cm) opening for elastic.

2. Cut elastic 4 3/4" (12cm) long. Using a small safety pin, insert elastic thru casing, gathering the fabric as you work the elastic thru. Overlap ends of elastic 1/4" (6mm) & hand-sew together securely.

3. Push elastic completely into casing and sew opening in facing closed.

4. For sleeve casings, press under 5/8" (15mm) on each sleeve edge. Sew 3/8" (8mm) from pressed edge.

5. Cut 2 pieces of elastic, each 2 1/2" (6cm) long. Using a small safety pin, insert elastic thru casings and sew securely at ends.

6. Press under 1/4" (6mm) on lower edge of RUFFLES. Sew 1/8" (3mm) from pressed edge.

7. To gather upper edge of ruffles, machine baste 1/4" and 1/8" (6mm and 3mm) from raw edge.

8. With RIGHT sides together, pin ruffles to lower edge of shirt front and shirt back, matching centers and having edges even. Pull up bobbin threads and adjust gathers to fit. Stitch in place. Press seam allowance toward shirt. On OUTSIDE, topstitch shirt 1/8" (3mm) from ruffle seam.

9. With RIGHT sides together, stitch entire underarm seam, pivoting needle at armpit. Clip seam allowance at armpit. ♥

PAJAMA PANTS

1. With RIGHT sides together, stitch center front seam. Clip curve.

2. For casing, press under 5/8" (15mm) on upper edge. Sew 3/8" (9mm) from pressed edge.

3. Cut elastic 4 1/2" (9cm) long. Using a small safety pin, insert elastic thru casing and sew securely at ends.

4. Press under 1/4" (6mm) on lower edge of RUFFLES. Sew 1/8" (3mm) from pressed edge.

5. To gather upper edge of ruffles, machine baste 1/4" and 1/8" (6mm and 3mm) from raw edge.

6. With RIGHT sides together, pin ruffles to pant legs, matching centers and having edges even. Pull up bobbin threads and adjust gathers to fit. Stitch in place. Press seam allowance toward pants. On OUTSIDE, topstitch pants 1/8" (3mm) from ruffle seam.

7. With RIGHT sides together, stitch center back seam. Clip curves.

8. With RIGHT sides together, stitch front to back at inner leg edges, matching center seams. ♥

SLIPPERS

1. Lay STRAP on top of SOLE so that ends of strap meet ends of tabs. Sew as shown by dotted lines in **Fig. A**.

2. Trim seam allowance close to stitchline as shown in **Fig. B**.

SLEEP MASK

1. Cut elastic 4" (10cm) long. Sew ends to sides of mask at DOTS (see pattern).

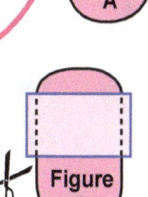

CAP-SLEEVE CROP TOP & WIDE-LEG PANTS

Faux-tweed tonal fabric was used for this outfit. It is quilt-weight cotton with subtle visual texture that is printed on.

Pictured with Bucket Bag, page 43.

SUPPLIES

Lightweight woven cotton or denim fabric, 1/4 yd (.23m)
3/4" (19mm) wide Velcro® Sleek & Thin™ sew-on tape
1 snap
All purpose glue stick, optional

Note: PATTERNS ARE ON PAGE 119. Pattern includes seam allowances. Seam allowances are 1/4" (6mm) unless instructions indicate otherwise.

CAP-SLEEVE TOP

1. With RIGHT sides together, stitch FRONT to BACKS at shoulder seams.

2. On neckline, stitch 1/4" (6mm) from edge. Press or glue* under on stitchline, clipping curves. Sew 1/8" (3mm) from turned edge.
* Note: To glue, lightly dab glue stick along wrong side of seam allowance and finger-press in place.

3. Make clips in side seams at DOTS (see pattern). Press under 1/4" (6mm) between dots to create armholes. Sew 1/8" from pressed edge.

4. With RIGHT sides together, stitch front to back at side seams.

5. Press under 1/4" (6mm) on lower edge of garment. Sew 1/8" (3mm) from pressed edge.

6. Apply fasteners; see FINISHING BACK OPENING EDGES, page 9, steps 1-6. ♥

WIDE-LEG PANTS

1. With RIGHT sides together, stitch center front seam of FRONT sections. Clip curve.

2. Sew darts on BACK sections. Press darts toward center.

3. With RIGHT sides together, sew fronts to backs at sides.

4. Pin WAISTBAND to upper edge of pants, RIGHT sides together, matching center fronts and back edges. Stitch. Trim seam allowance to 1/8" 3mm). Press seam toward waistband.

5.. Fold waistband along foldline (see pattern) over seam allowance to inside of pants. On OUTSIDE, topstitch waistband close to seam thru all layers.

6. Press under 1/4" (6mm) on lower edge of pants. Sew 1/8" (3mm) from pressed edge.

7. With RIGHT sides together, sew center back seam of pants back sections BETWEEN DOTS with **1/2" (1.2cm)** seam allowance, leaving an opening above dots. Trim seam allowance to 1/4" between dots. Clip curve.

8. With RIGHT sides together, stitch fronts to backs at inner leg edges matching crotch seams. Clip seam allowance on each side of crotch.

9. Press under 1/2" (1.2cm) on one back opening edge. Sew prong half of snap to INSIDE on waistband. Sew socket half of snap to OUTSIDE on opposite edge. ♥

SWEATER DRESS & HAT

These garments are made from socks. The dress features raglan sleeves and a wide, rolled collar. If your socks have a pattern, such as the Fair Isle design used here, be sure to plan your cutting so the stripes match at the seams. I found it easiest to place the pattern pieces by cutting the socks open along the center back, cutting off the toes, and opening them up into flat pieces.

Fusible tape is used in the hem of the dress. This is the best way to get a smooth hem on stretchy fabric. The one I used is SewkeysE "Extremely Fine Double Sided Fusible Stay Tape". Follow the instructions included with your particular product.

Pictured with Footless Stockings, page 25.

SUPPLIES

1 pair lightweight socks, womens' crew or knee length

Double-sided fusible tape, 1/4" (6mm) wide

3 snaps

Note: PATTERN IS ON PAGE 121. Pattern includes seam allowances. Seam allowances are 1/4" (6mm) unless instructions indicate otherwise.

DRESS

1. At lower edge of each SLEEVE, press fusible tape to WRONG side along raw edge. Peel paper backing from fusible tape. Press under 1/4" (6mm) hem. Sew over raw edge using a zigzag stitch at a *long wide* setting.

2. With RIGHT sides together, stitch armhole edges of sleeves to armhole edges of DRESS FRONT and DRESS BACK.

3. Fold COLLAR in half lengthwise with WRONG sides together. Zigzag raw edges together.

```
COLLAR
FOLDLINE
```

4. Pin zigzag edge of collar to neckline at WRONG side of garment, matching centers, having back edges even and stretching dress to fit. Sew in place, 1/8" (3mm) from edge, using a zigzag stitch at a *long wide* setting.

5. With RIGHT sides together, stitch entire seam of underarms and sides.

6. At lower edge of sweater, press fusible tape to WRONG side along raw edge. Peel paper backing from fusible tape. Press under 1/4" (6mm) hem. Sew over raw edge using a zigzag stitch at a *long wide* setting.

Note: Try sweater on doll before Step 7 and adjust seam allowance, if needed, for best fit.

7. With RIGHT sides together, sew up center back, **1/2" (1.2cm)** from edge, stitching from hem to DOT (see pattern).

8. Flip collar to outside of garment. To secure, sew ends of collar to edges of dress with zigzag.

9. Turn under 1/2" (1.2cm) on one back opening edge. Sew prong half of snap to INSIDE of this edge. Sew socket half of snap to OUTSIDE of opposite edge. ♥

Tip: *To make dressing easier, slip small plastic covers over the doll's hands. These can be made by cutting triangles from the corners of a sandwich bag.*

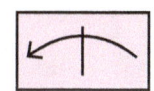

HAT

Cut a 4"x6" (10x15cm) rectangle of sock fabric.

1. Fold HAT in half widthwise with RIGHT sides together. Stitch center back seam.

2. With hat WRONG-SIDE out, hand-gather with 1 row of running stitch around top of hat, 1/4" (6mm) from edge, using a double strand of thread. Pull up gathers tight, wrap thread around gathers several times and secure with a knot.

3. For brim, on bottom of hat, turn 1 1/4" (3cm) to WRONG side. **Sew in place by hand with whip stitch over raw edge.**

Turn hat right side out.

Fold up brim. ♥

OPEN-FRONT JACKET

Faux leather gives this pattern a luxe look. I used fabric from a retired purse to make the jacket pictured. It is layered it over a Shell, page 35.

See page 6 for tips on working with faux leather.

The Open-Front Jacket is a versatile garment that is suitable for cotton fabric, too.

SUPPLIES

Lightweight faux-leather or woven fabric, 1/4 yd (.23m)

Note: PATTERN IS ON PAGE 125. Pattern includes seam allowances. Seam allowances are 1/4" (6mm) unless instructions indicate otherwise.

1. With RIGHT sides together, stitch FRONT to BACK at shoulder seams.

2. On jacket back, clip curves of neckline, being careful not to clip beyond seam allowance. Turn under 1/4" (6mm) along entire edge of fronts and neckline. Sew 1/8" (3mm) from turned edge.

3. Turn under 1/4" (6mm) on lower edge of sleeves. Sew 1/8" (3mm) from turned edge.

4. With RIGHT sides together, sew sleeves to armhole edge of jacket, matching DOT (see pattern) to shoulder seam.

5. With RIGHT sides together, stitch front to back at entire underarm seam, matching the armhole seams.

6. Turn up 1/4" (6mm) on lower edge of jacket. Sew 1/8" from turned edge. ♥

FLARE-LEG JEANS

Use gold thread for the decorative topstitching.

SUPPLIES

Lightweight denim fabric, 1/4 yd (.23m)

1 snap

Note: PATTERN IS ON PAGE 123. Pattern includes seam allowances. Seam allowances are 1/4" (6mm) unless instructions indicate otherwise.

1. Sew darts on JEANS BACK sections. Press darts toward center.

2. For mock pockets, topstitch JEANS FRONTS as shown on pattern with dashed lines.

3. With RIGHT sides together, stitch fronts to backs at sides. Press seam toward back.

4. On OUTSIDE, topstitch backs along side seams, sewing 1/8" (3mm) from the seam.

5. With RIGHT sides together, stitch center front seam of jeans front sections. Clip curve.

6. On OUTSIDE, topstitch along *one side* of center front seam, sewing 1/8" (3mm) from the seam.

7. To staystitch waistline, sew 1/4" (6mm) from edge. Clip to stitching. Press under on stitchline and topstitch 1/8" (3mm) from pressed edge.

8. Press under 1/4" (6mm) hem on bottom of pant legs. Topstitch 1/8" (3mm) from pressed edges.

9. With RIGHT sides together, sew center back seam of jeans back sections BETWEEN DOTS with **1/2" (1.2cm)** seam allowance, leaving an opening above dots. Trim seam allowance to 1/4" (6mm) between dots. Clip curve.

10. With RIGHT sides together, stitch fronts to backs at inner leg edges, matching crotch seams. Clip seam allowance on each side of crotch.

11. Press under 1/2" (1.2cm) on one back opening edge. Sew prong half of snap to INSIDE of this edge. Sew socket half of snap to OUTSIDE of opposite edge. ♥

RUCHED PURSE

This purse is made from woven cotton fabric, so you can have fun using prints as well as solids! I especially love this pattern because I carried a silver purse in this style at my son's wedding ♡

SUPPLIES
Lightweight woven cotton fabric
1 snap
Fabric glue, optional

Note: PATTERN IS ON PAGE 125. Pattern includes seam allowances. Seam allowances are 1/4" (6mm) unless instructions indicate otherwise.

1. To gather upper and lower edges of PURSE, machine baste 1/4" and 1/8" (6mm and 3mm) from raw edge between DOTS (see pattern).

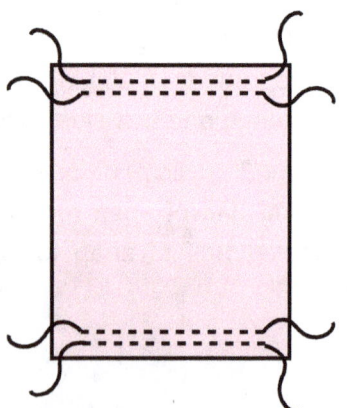

2. Pull up bobbin threads and adjust gathers into 1 1/2" (3.8cm). Fasten gathering threads securely on each side by knotting thread tails together.

3. Press under 1/4" (6mm) on gathered edges. Sew 1/8" (3mm) from pressed edges.

4. With RIGHT sides together, fold purse on foldline (see pattern). Stitch sides.

5. Turn right-side out. Finger press.

6. Press under 1/4" (6mm) on both long edges of HANDLE. Fold handle in half lengthwise, WRONG sides together, and press again. Sew close to both lengthwise edges.

7. Lap upper side edges of purse 3/8" (9mm) over ends of handle, being careful not to twist handle. Sew or glue handle in place.

8. Sew snap to inside of purse at upper edge with prong half of snap at center front and socket half at center back. ♥

FULL-SIZE PATTERNS

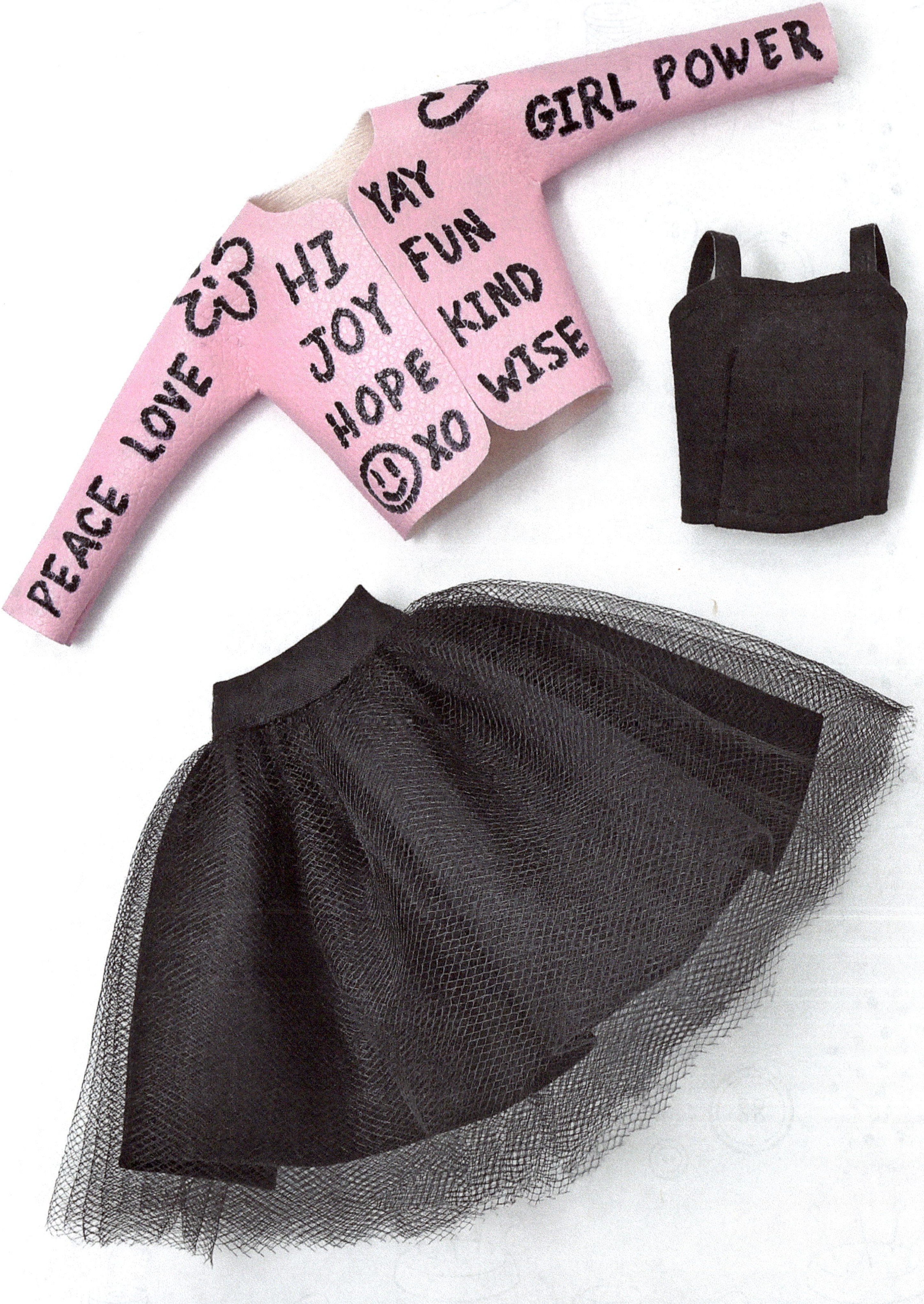
GIRL POWER
YAY
FUN
KIND
WISE
HI
JOY
HOPE
XO
PEACE LOVE

GRAFFITI JACKET
From Page 11
Full-Size Pattern

Cut 1 of Faux Leather

GRAFFITI JACKET

© 2025 Lindaloo Enterprises

HOW TO TRACE GRAFFITI ONTO FAUX LEATHER

If your faux-leather is a light color that is see-through enough, you can trace the graphics onto your fabric using a Light Box or a sunny window:

- With a Light Box, place pattern under piece of faux leather and trace.
- With a window, staple the full 8.5" x 11" pattern page to the edges of faux leather piece. Tape this to a window and trace.

TUTU SKIRT & BUSTIER
From Page 11
Full-Size Patters

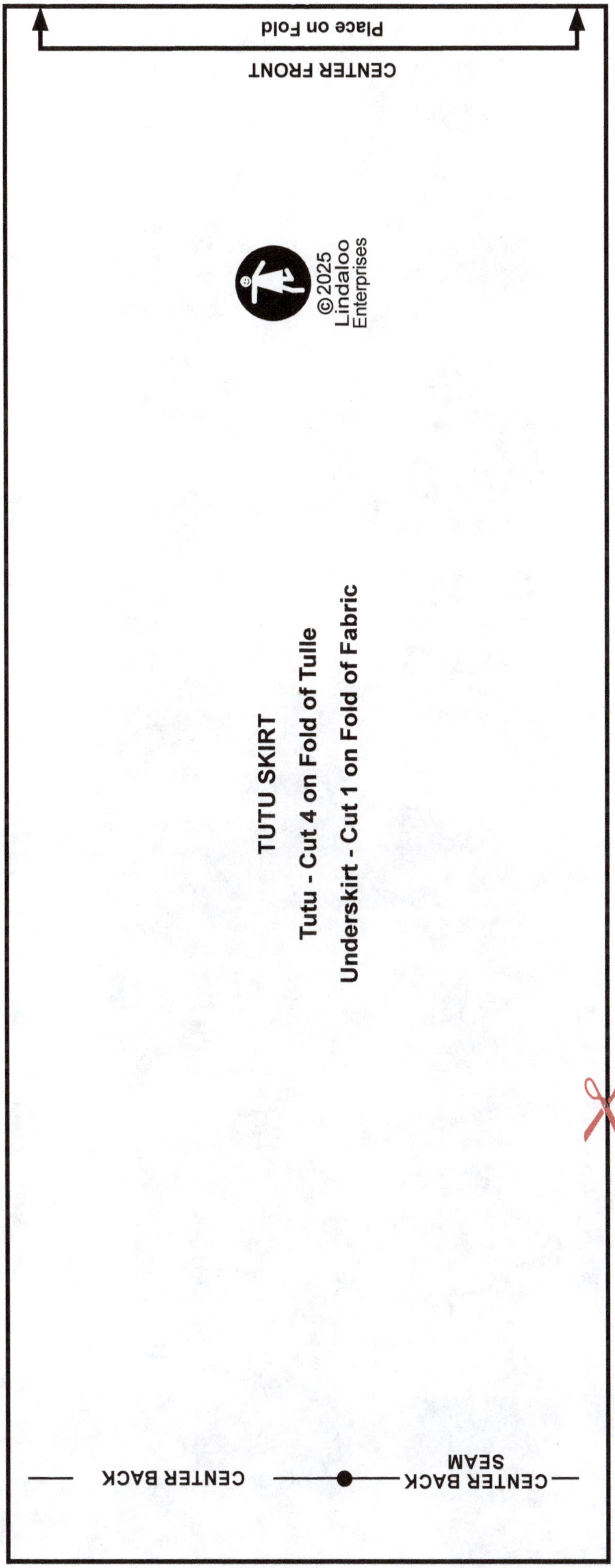

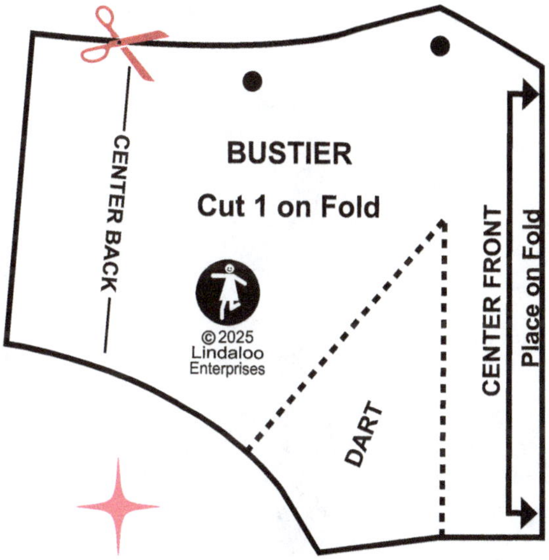

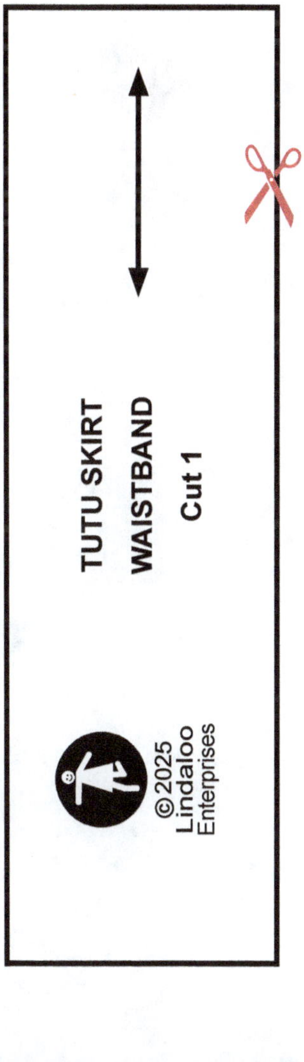

Place on Fold
CENTER FRONT
©2025
Lindaloo
Enterprises
TUTU SKIRT
Tutu - Cut 4 on Fold of Tulle
Underskirt - Cut 1 on Fold of Fabric
CENTER BACK
CENTER BACK
SEAM

BUSTIER
Cut 1 on Fold
CENTER BACK
©2025
Lindaloo
Enterprises
DART
CENTER FRONT
Place on Fold

TUTU SKIRT
WAISTBAND
Cut 1
©2025
Lindaloo
Enterprises

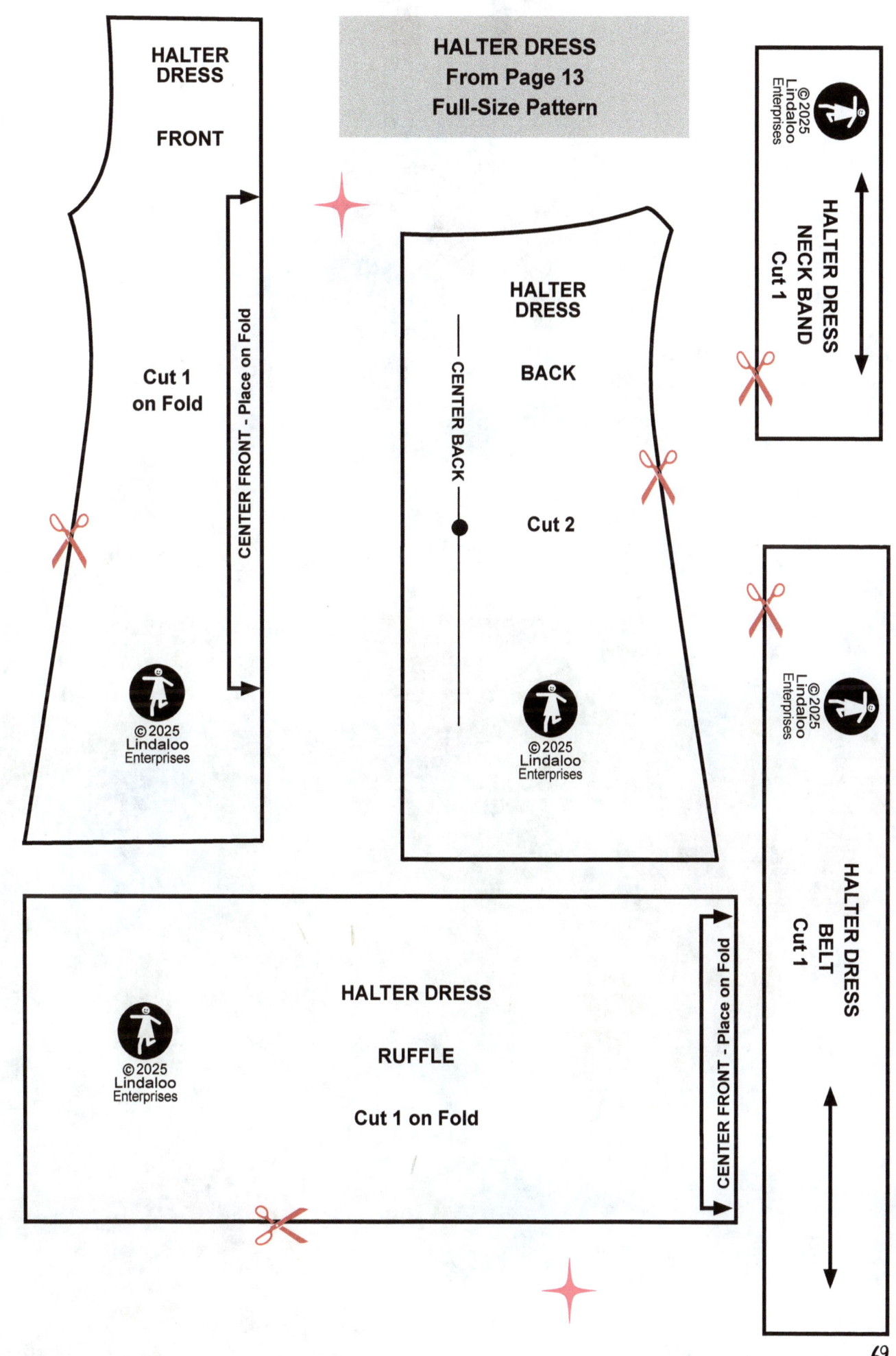

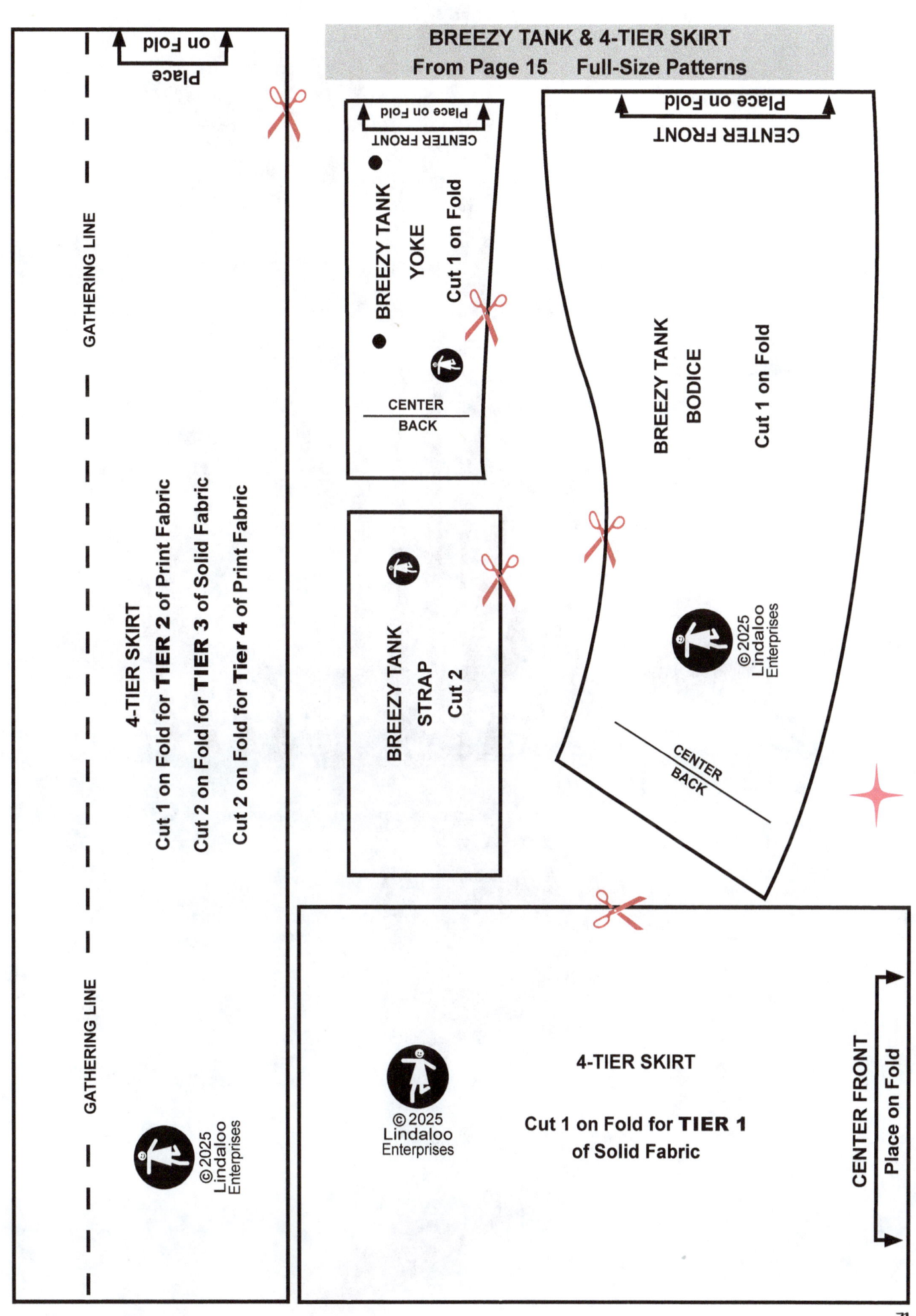

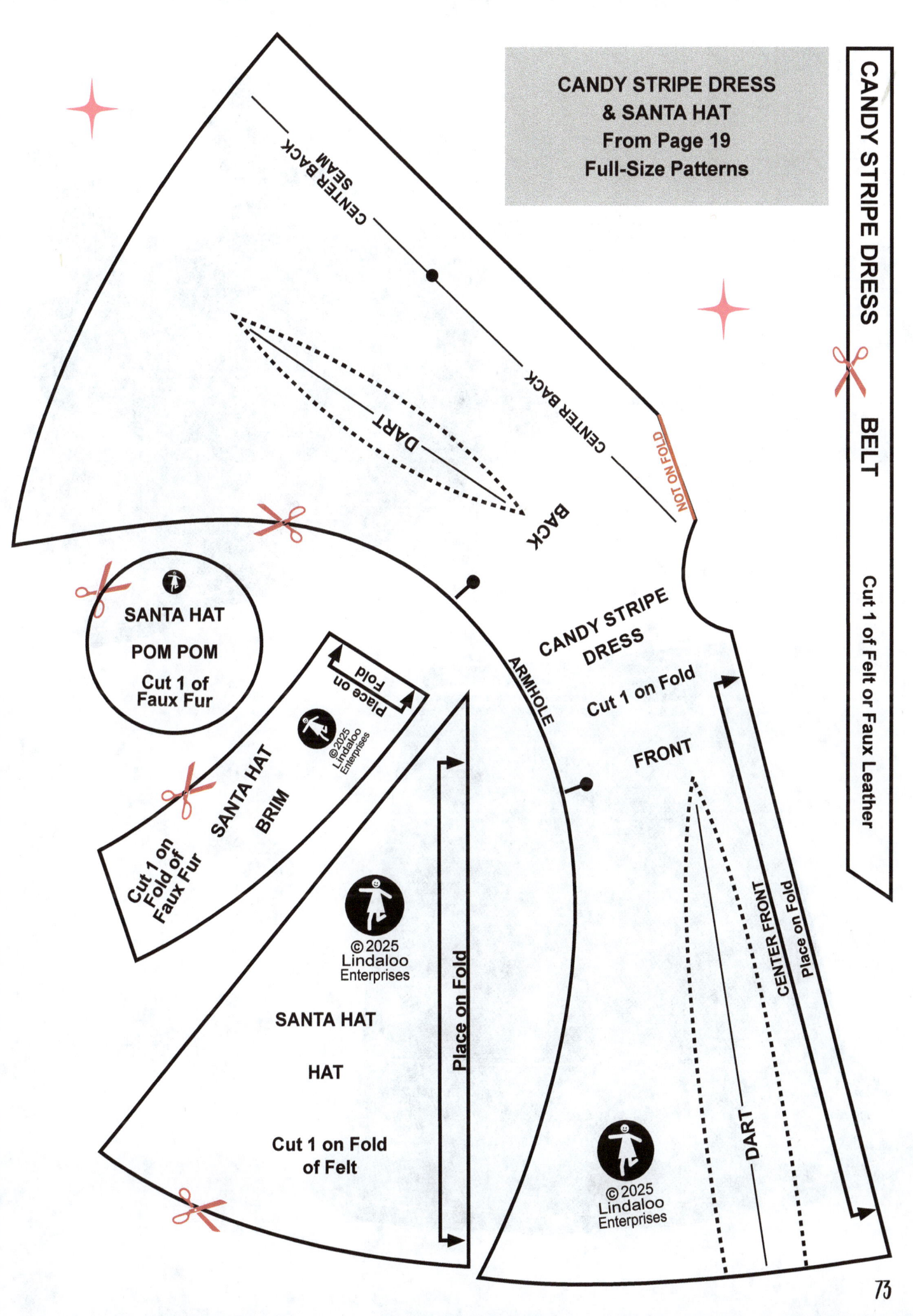

FRILLED CAMISOLE & SKIRT
From Page 21
Full-Size Patterns

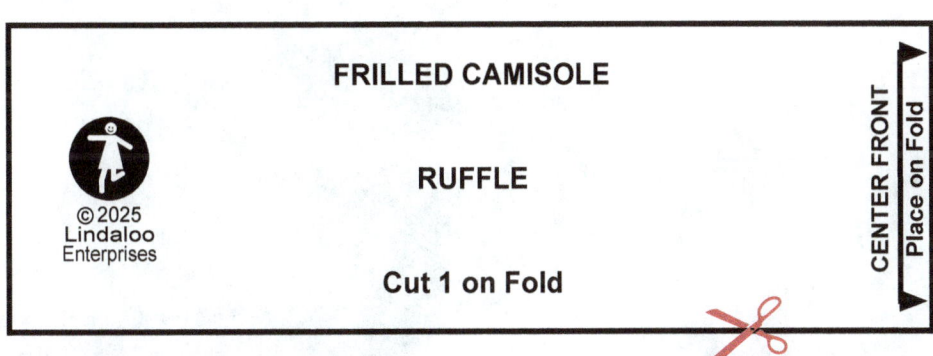

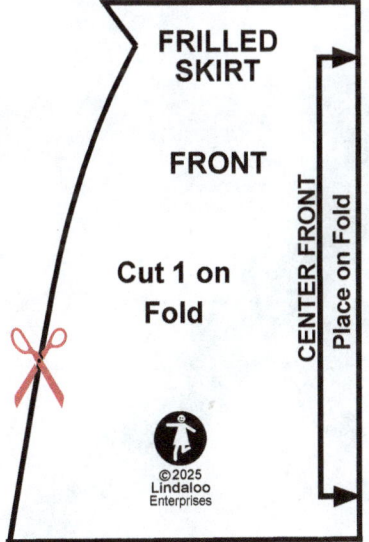

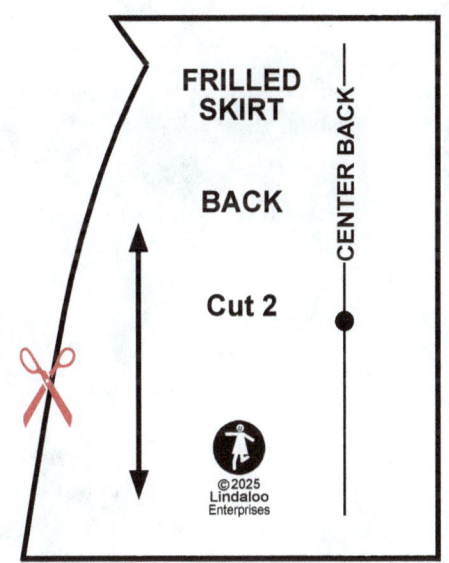

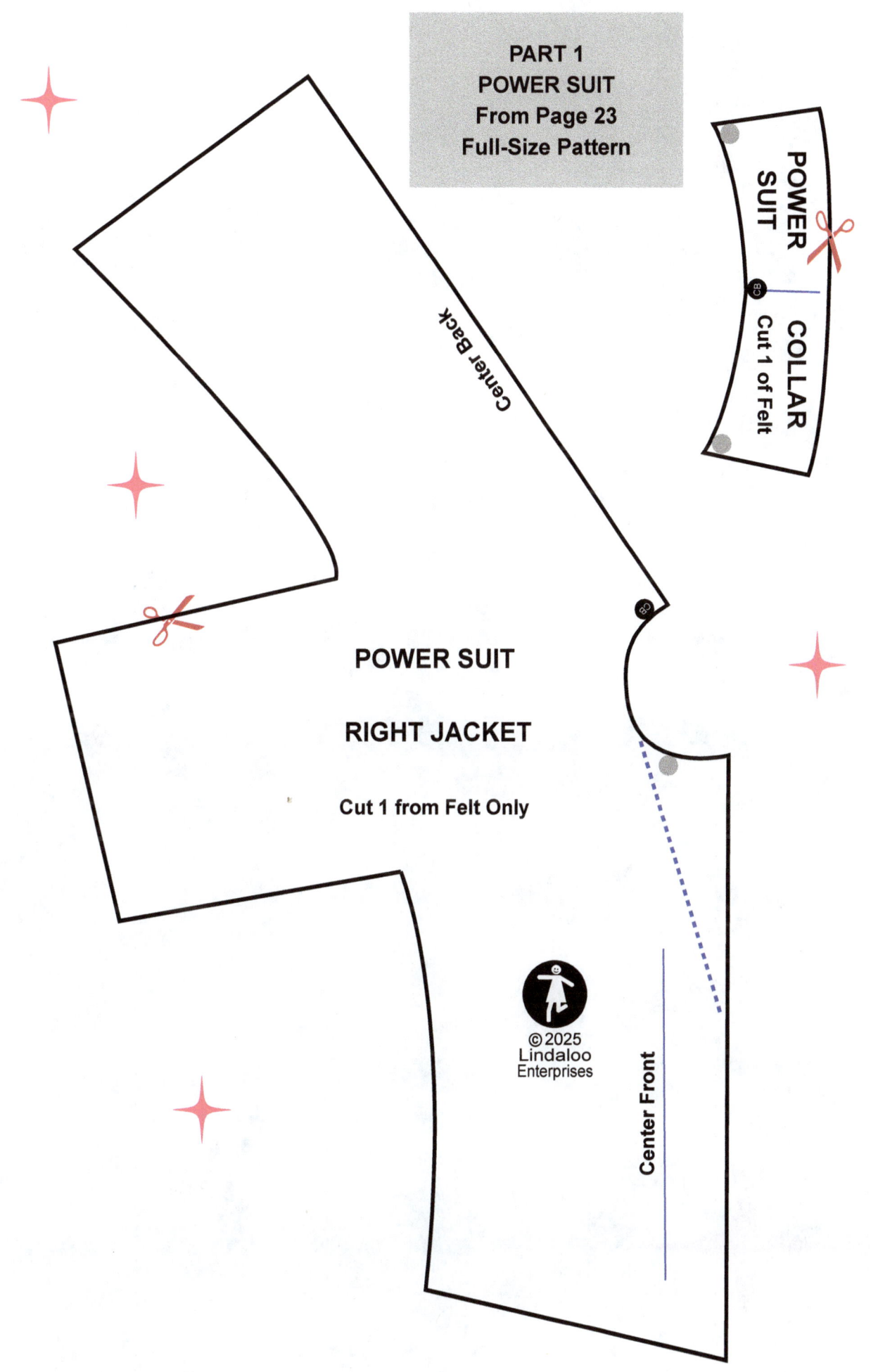

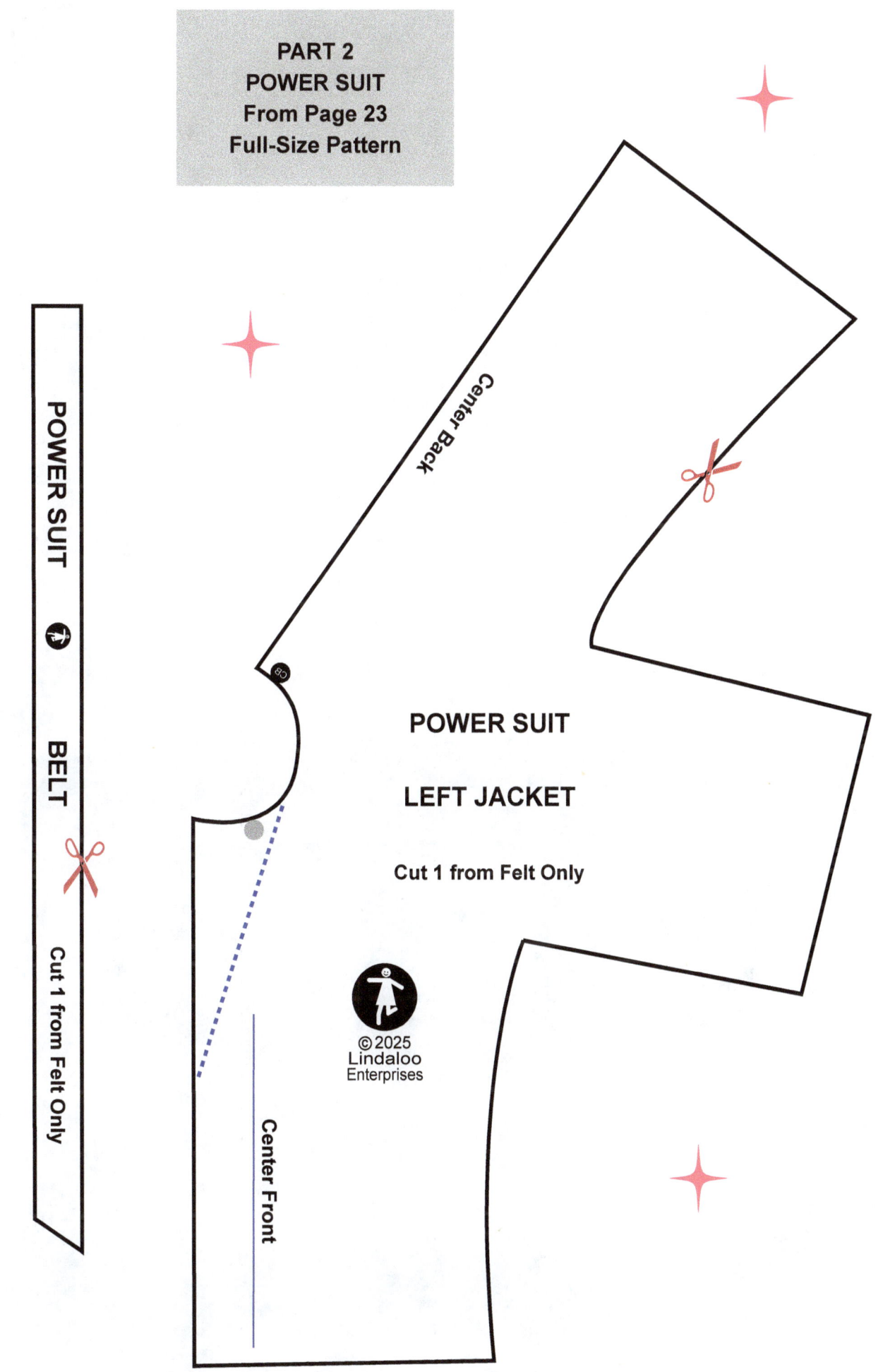

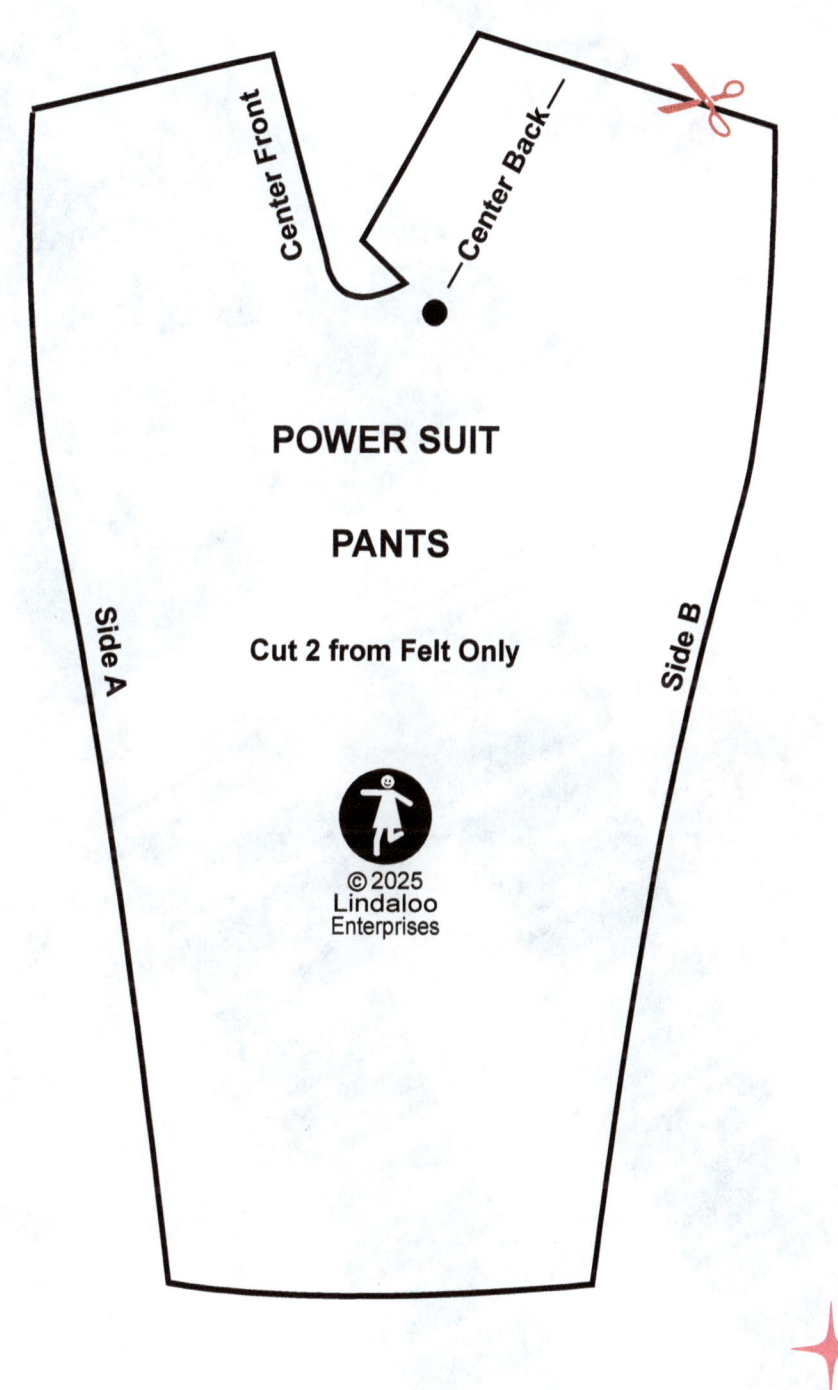

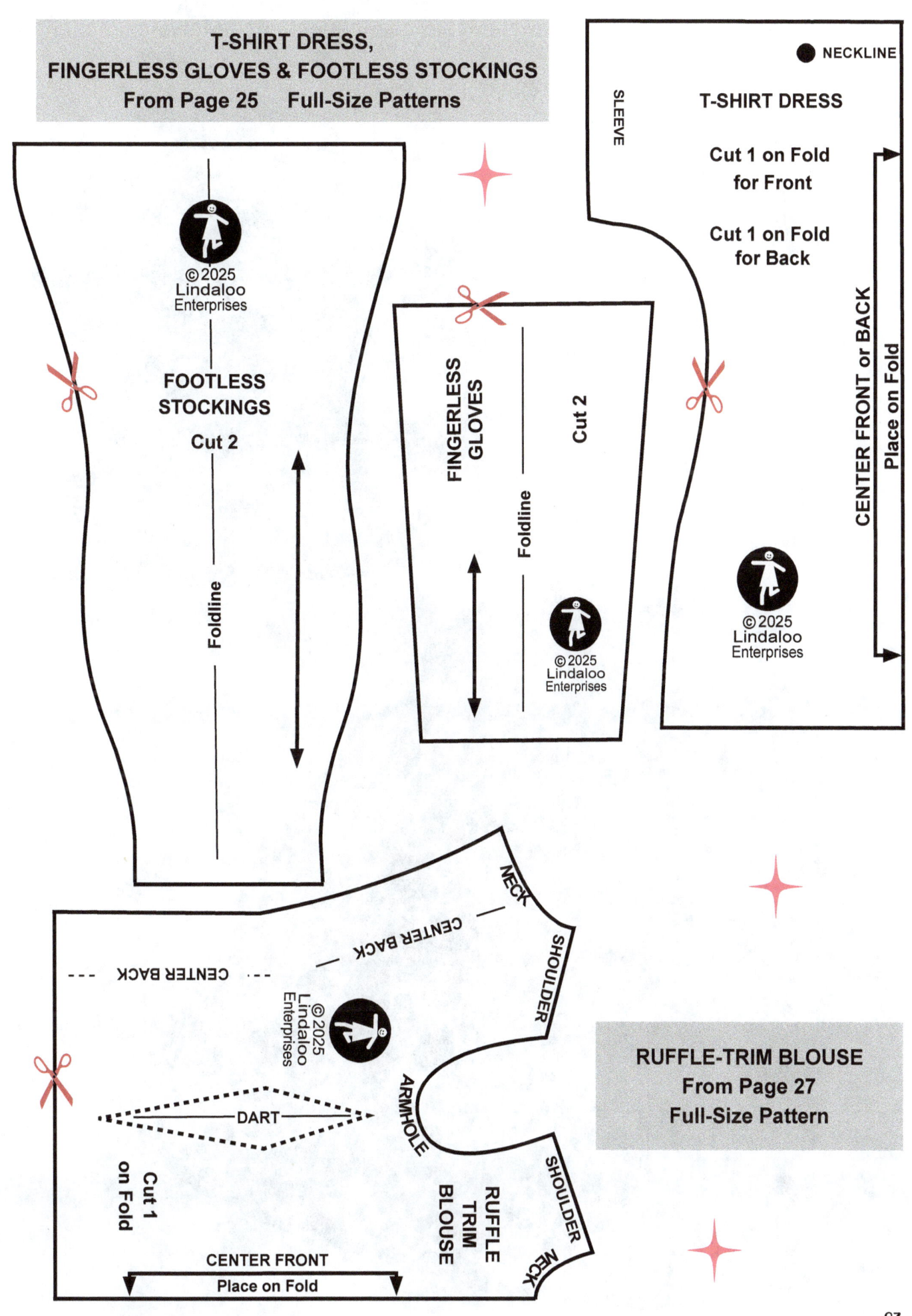

FULL SKIRT
From Page 27   Full-Size Pattern
(Blouse pattern is on previous page)

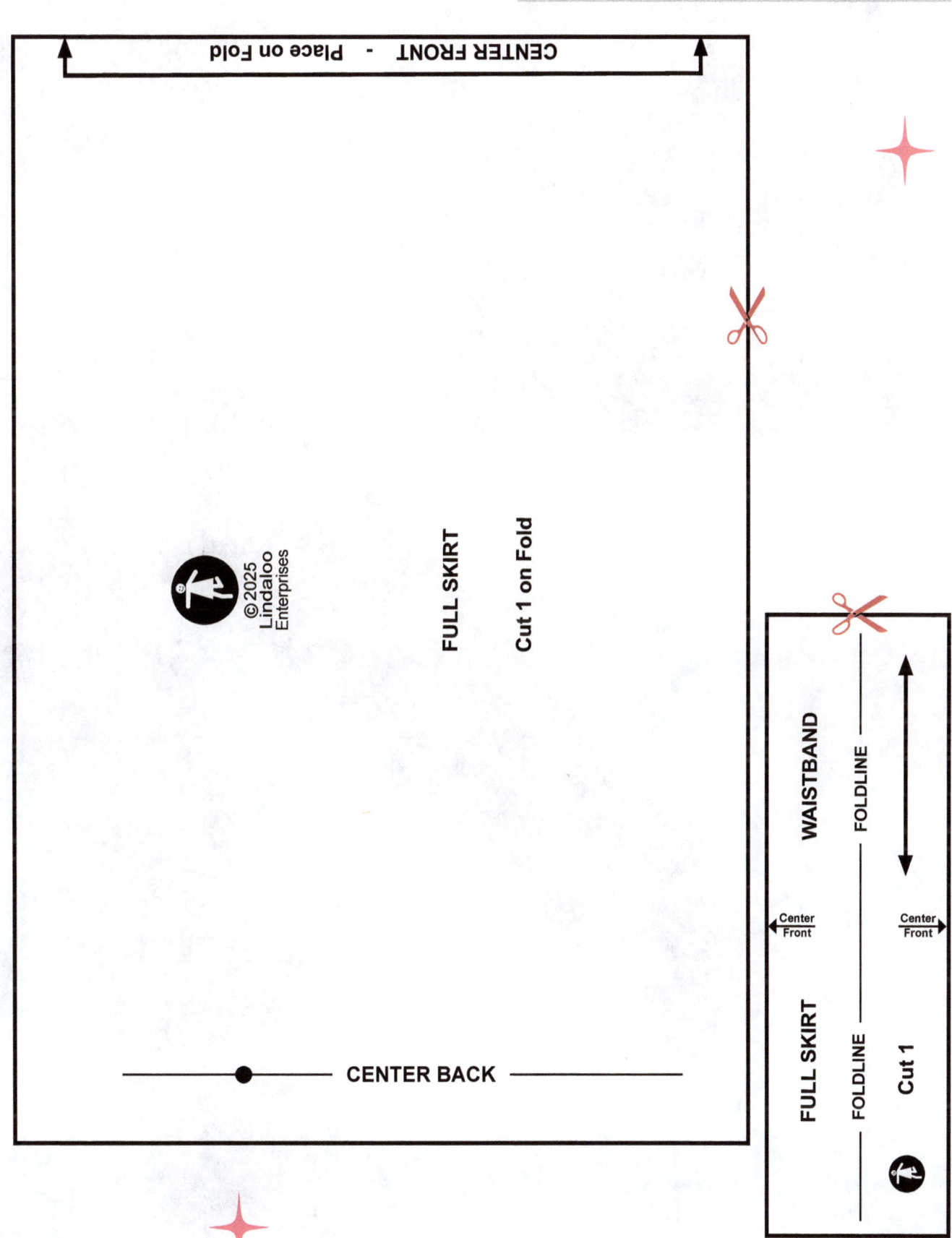

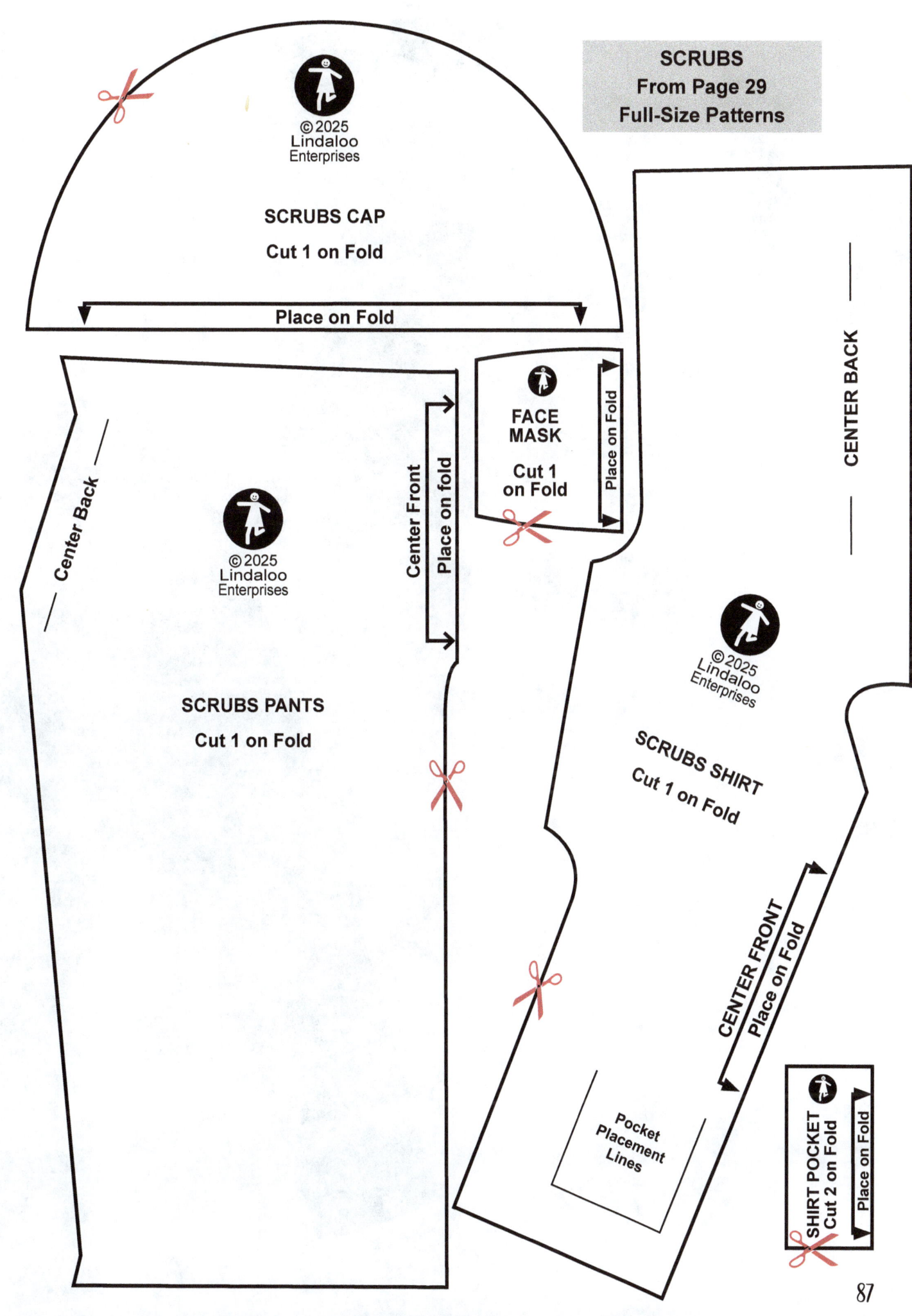

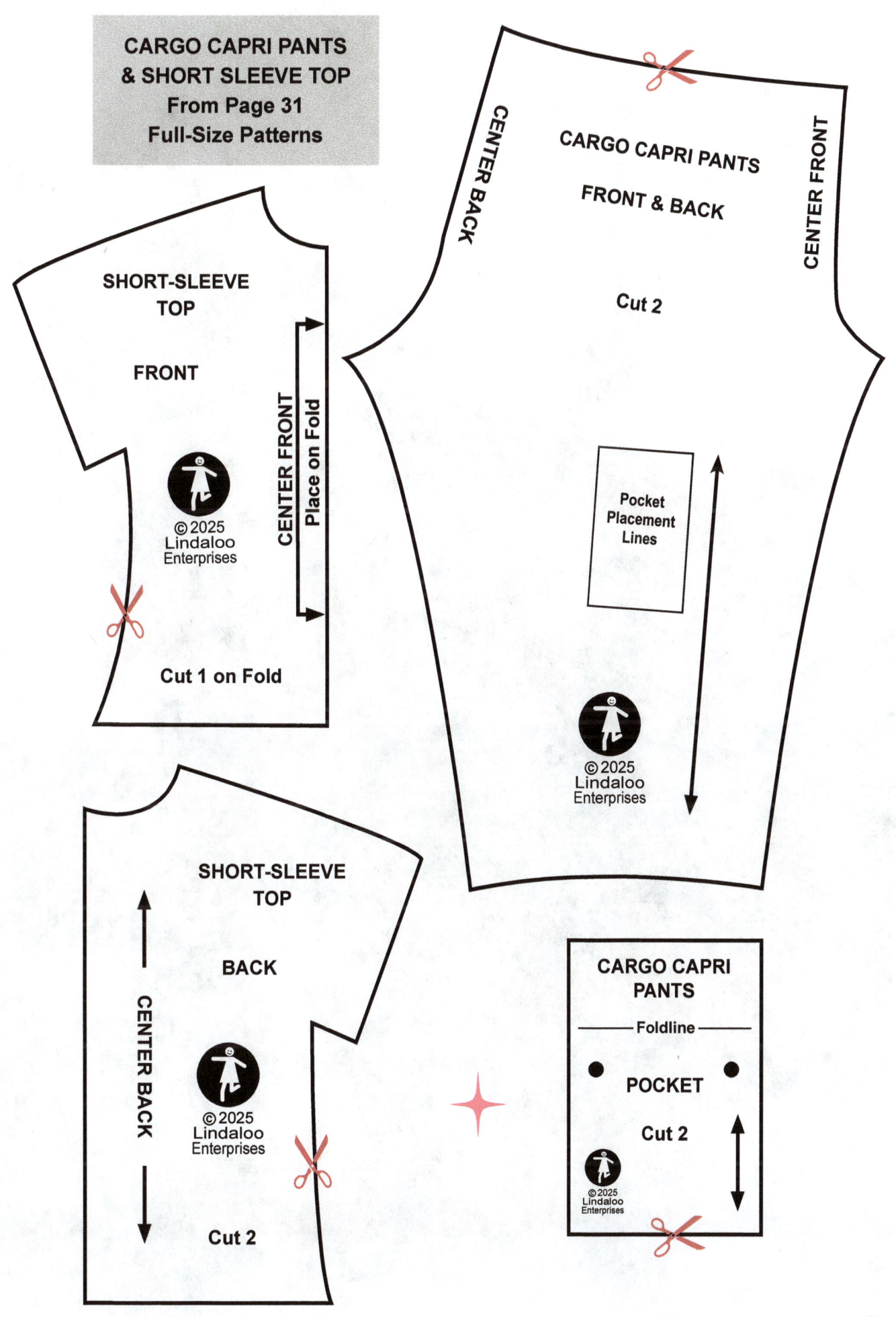

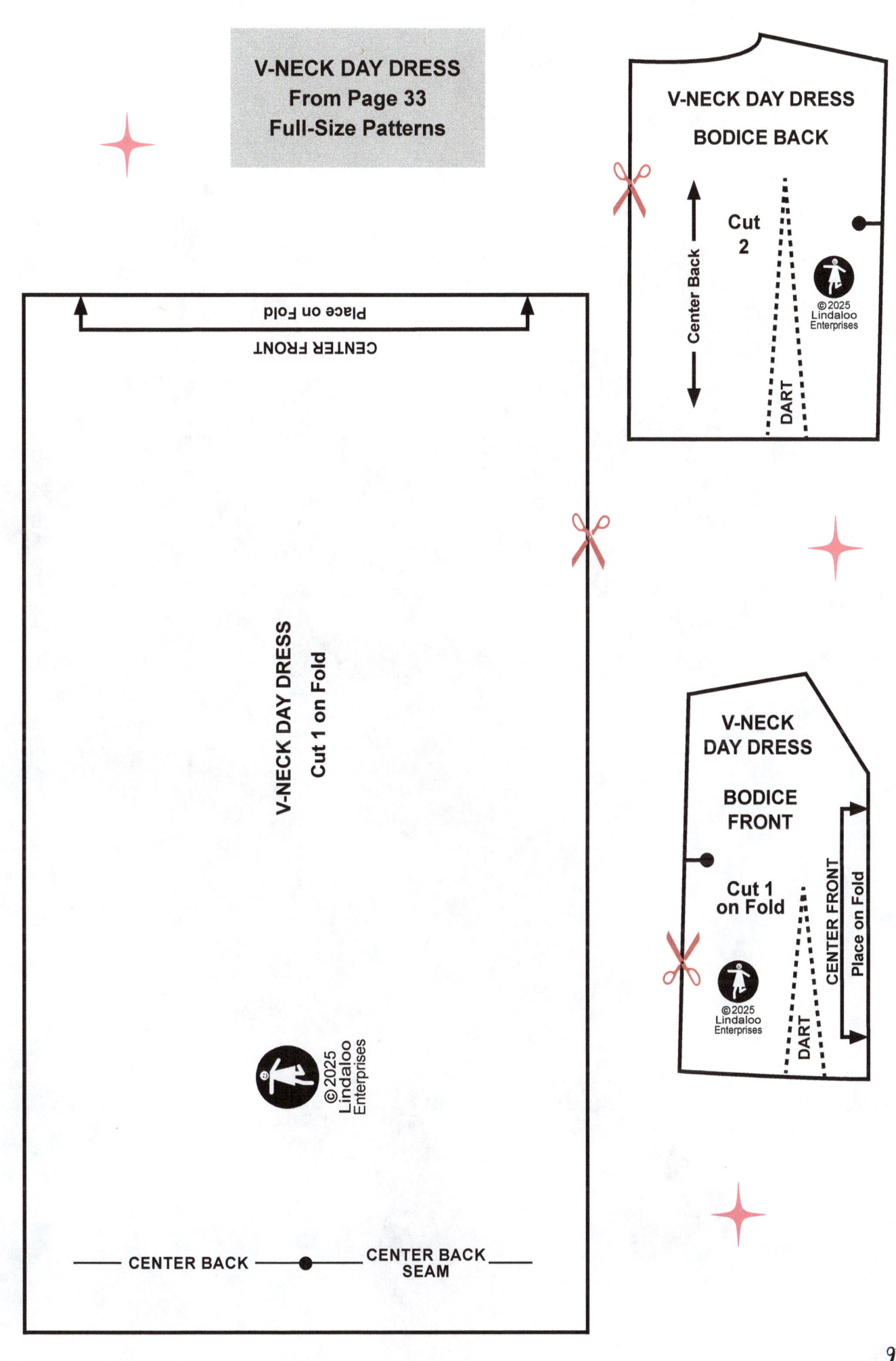

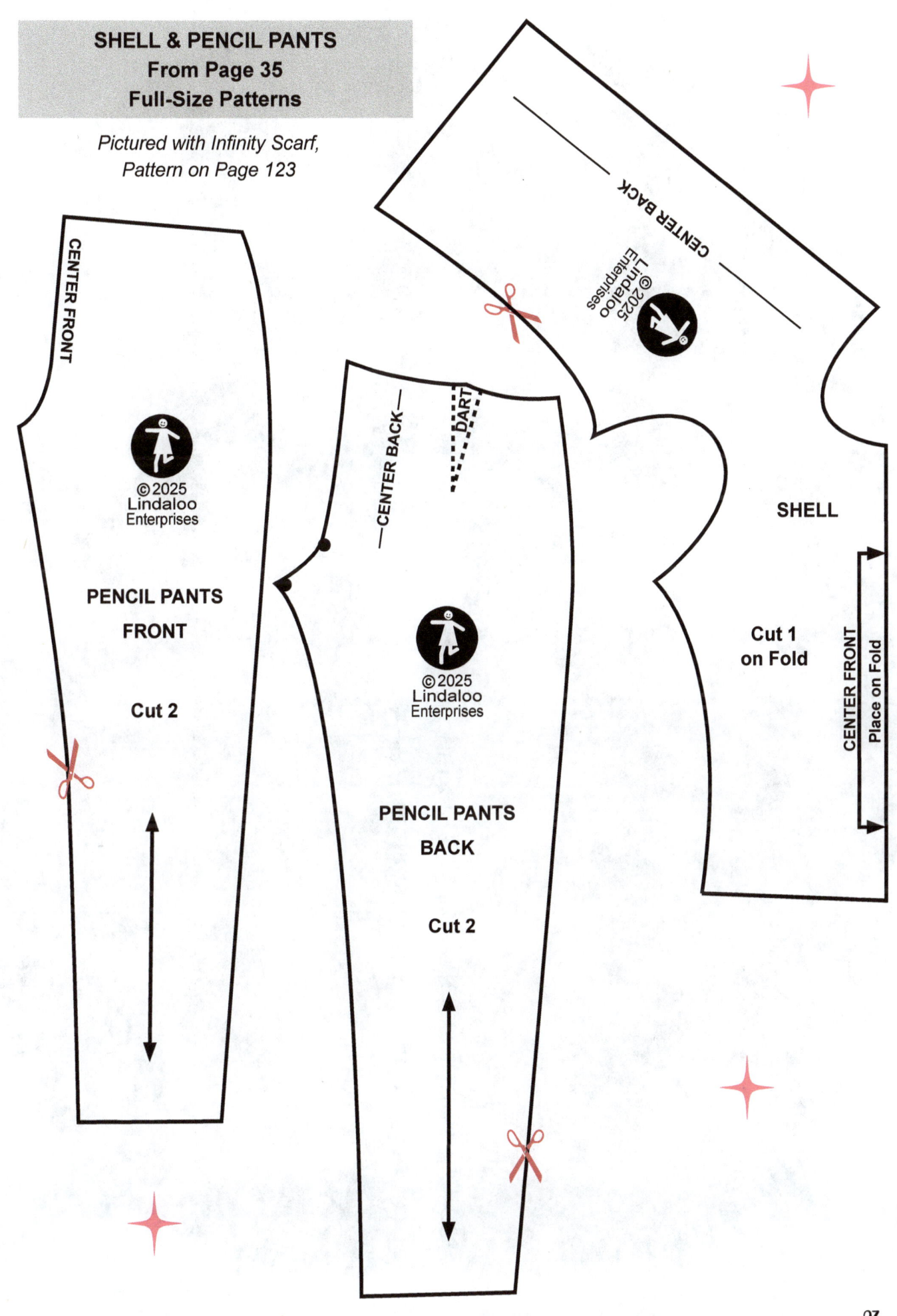

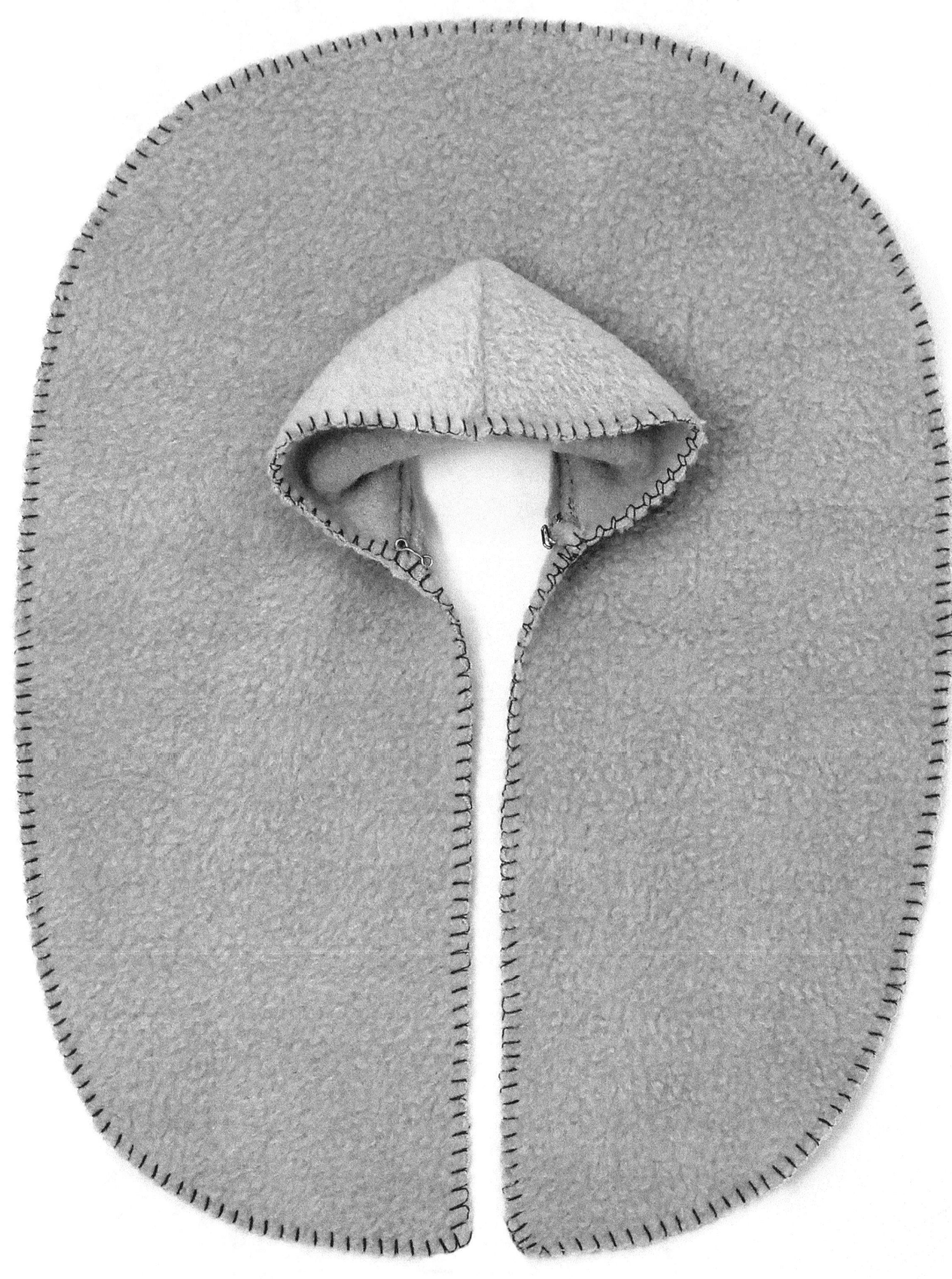

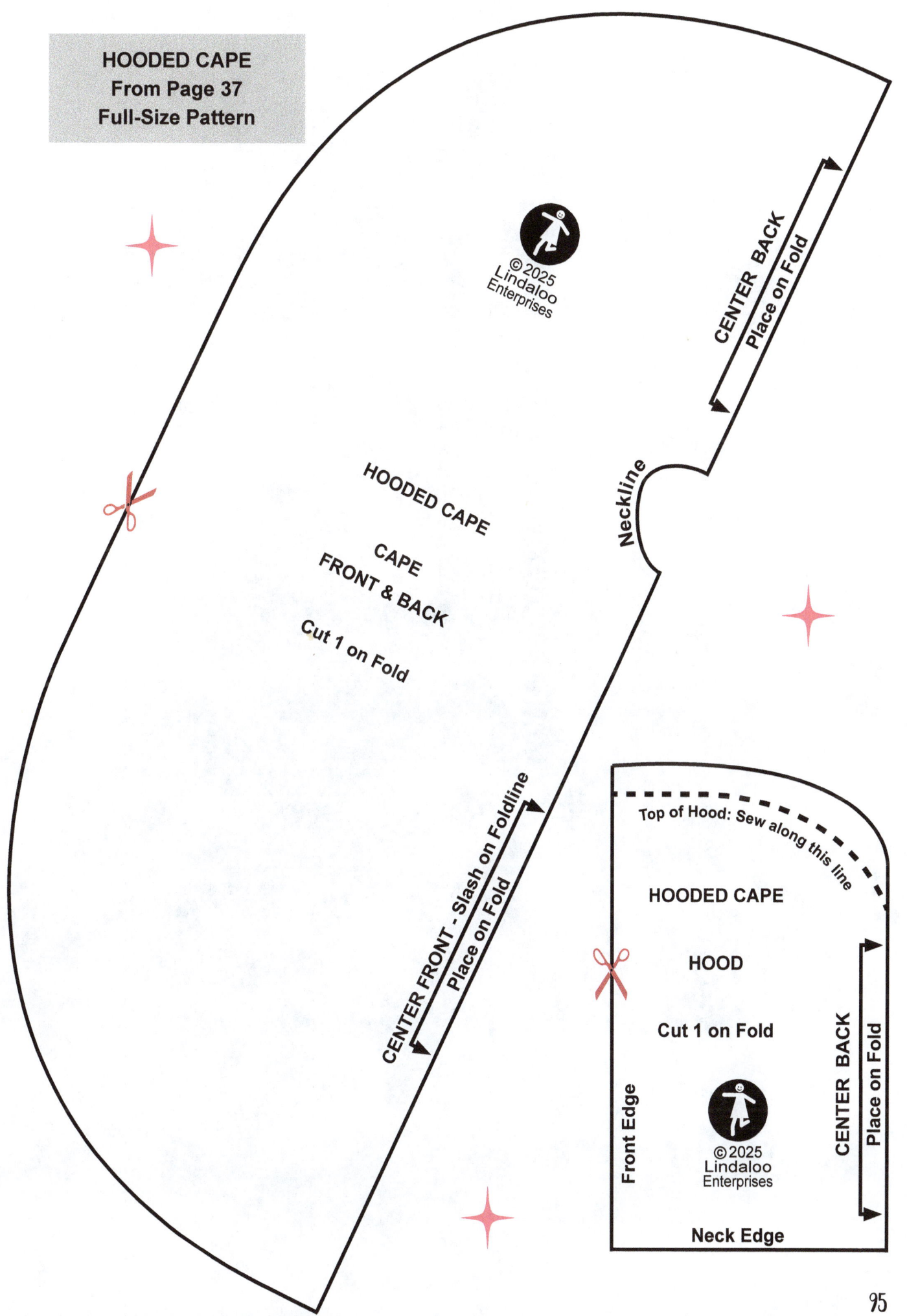

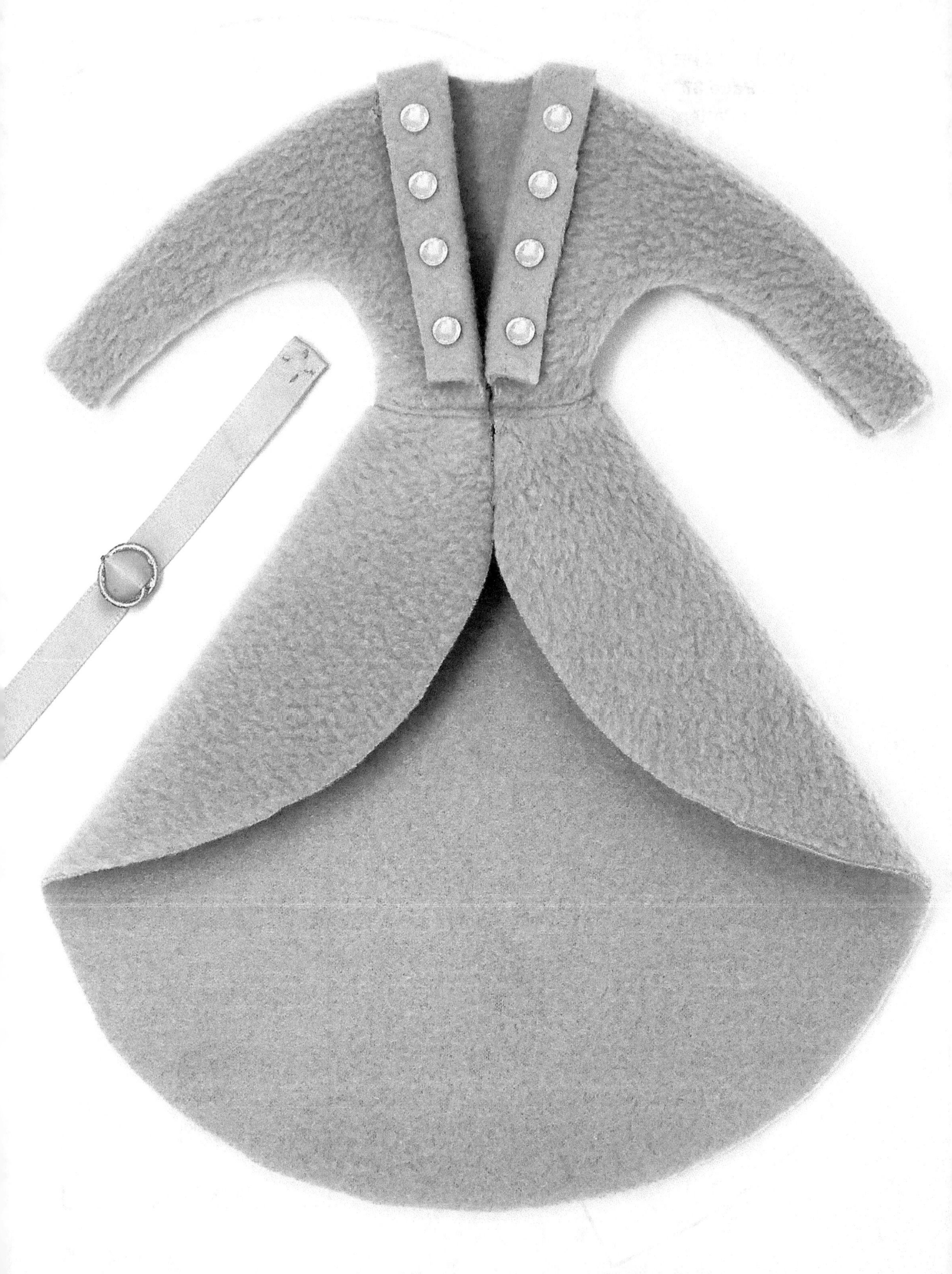

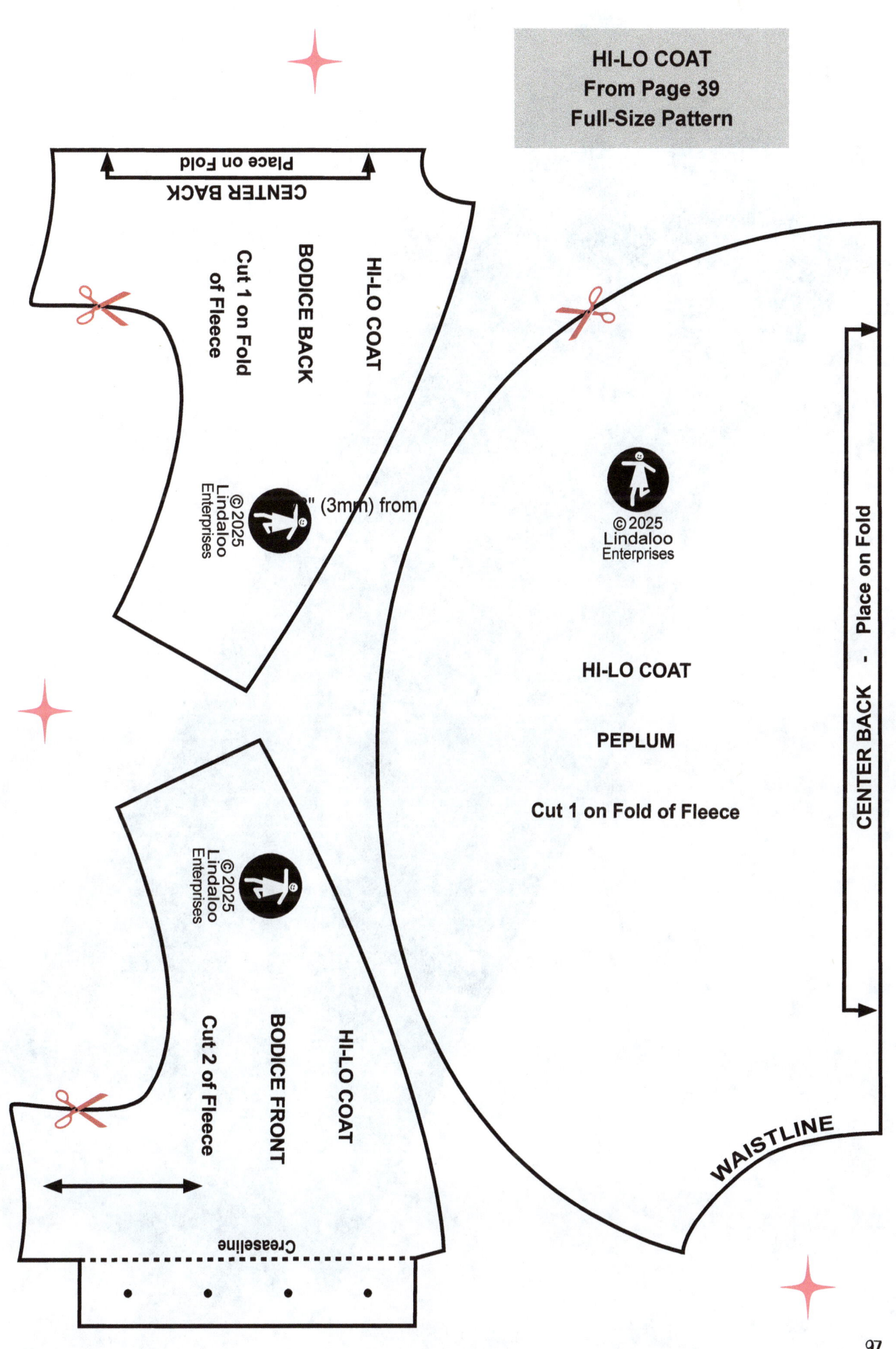

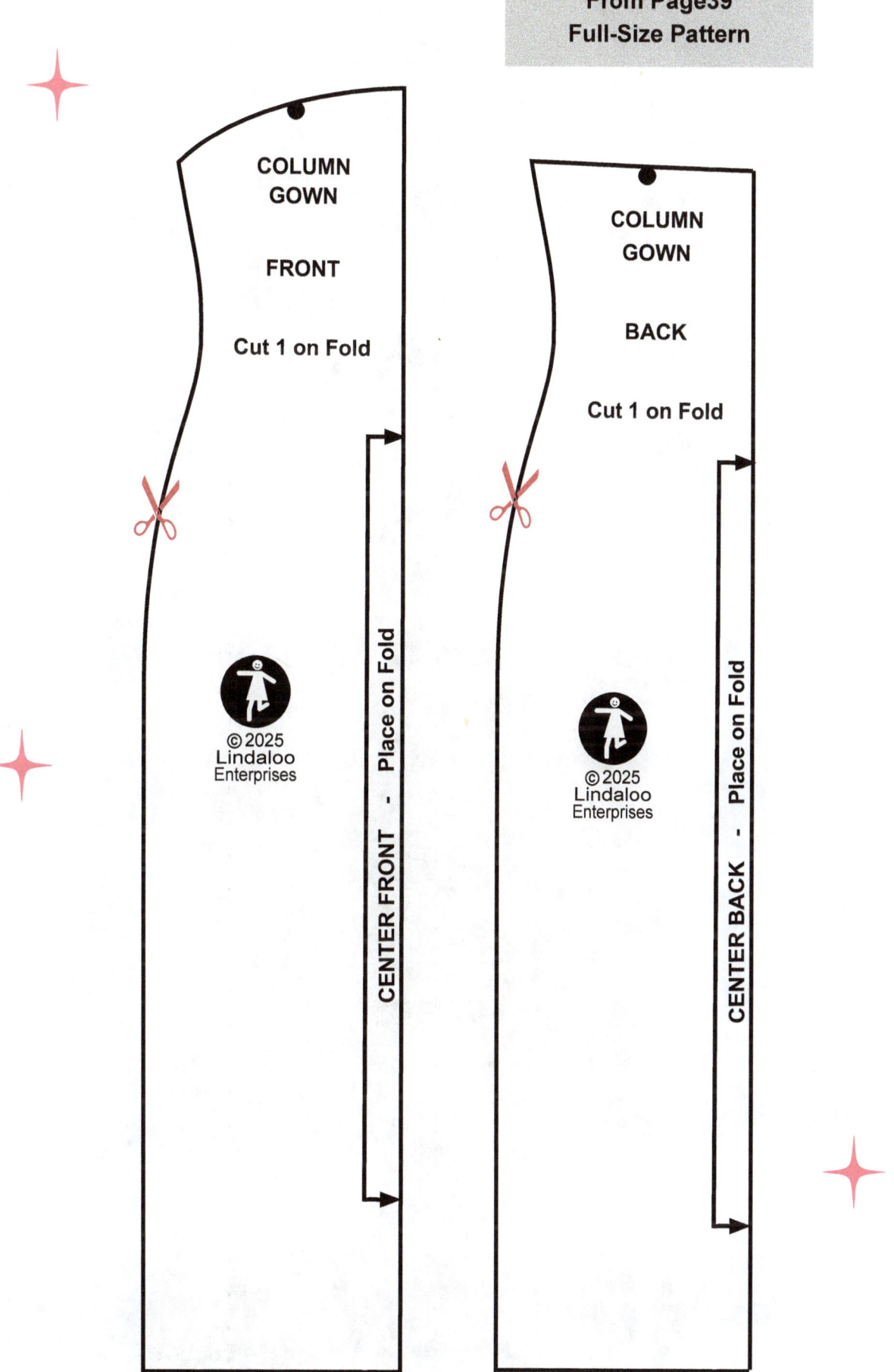

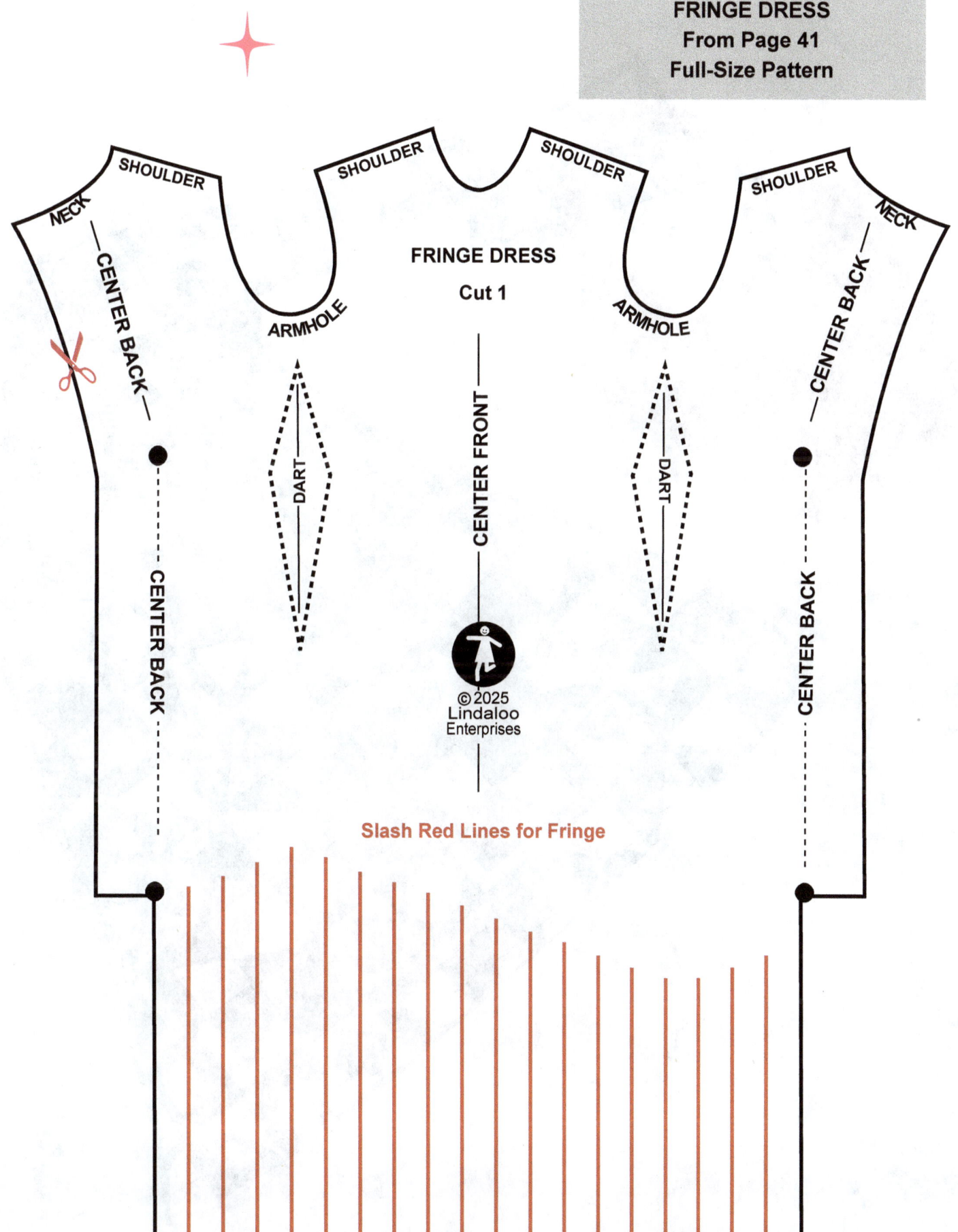

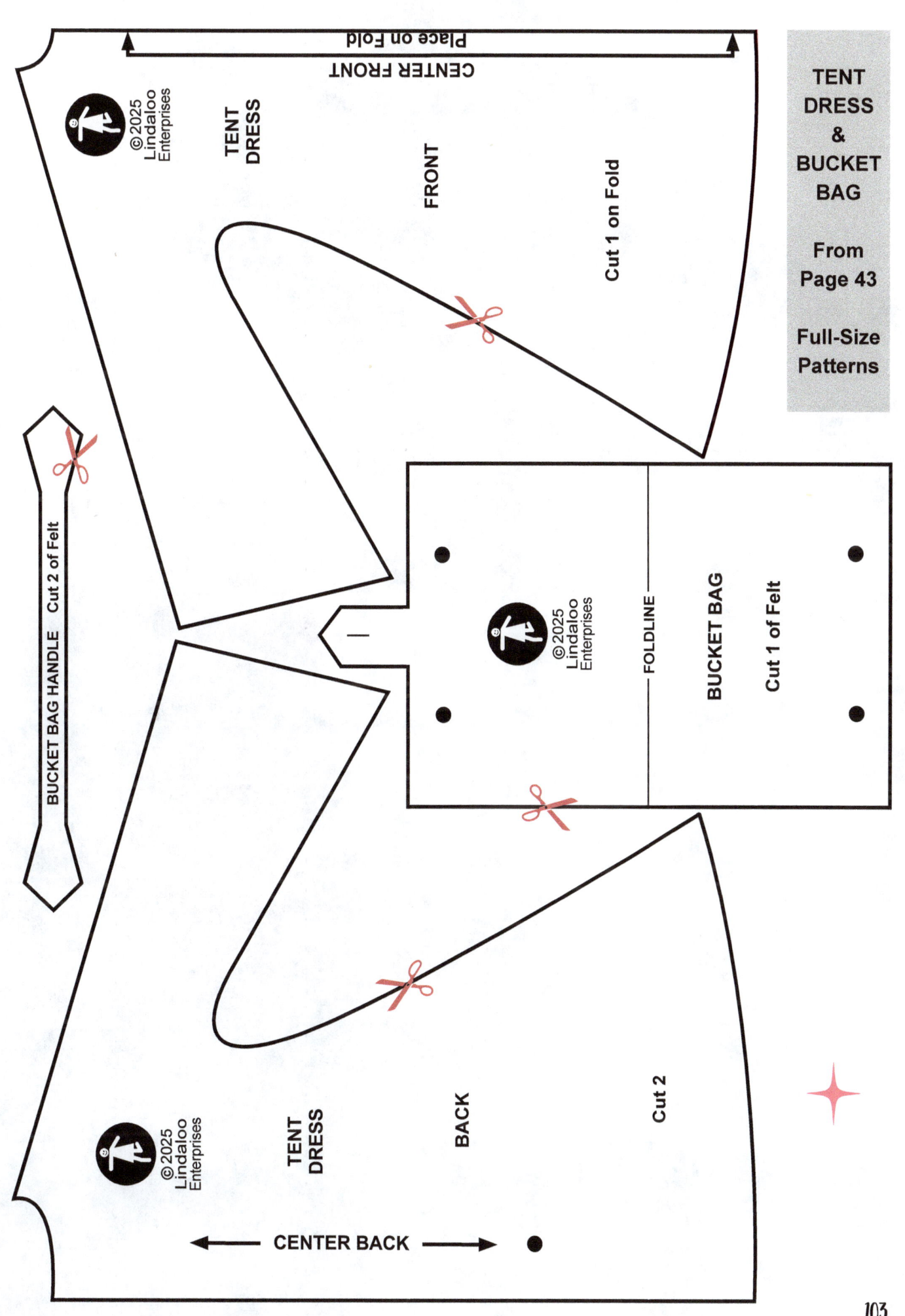

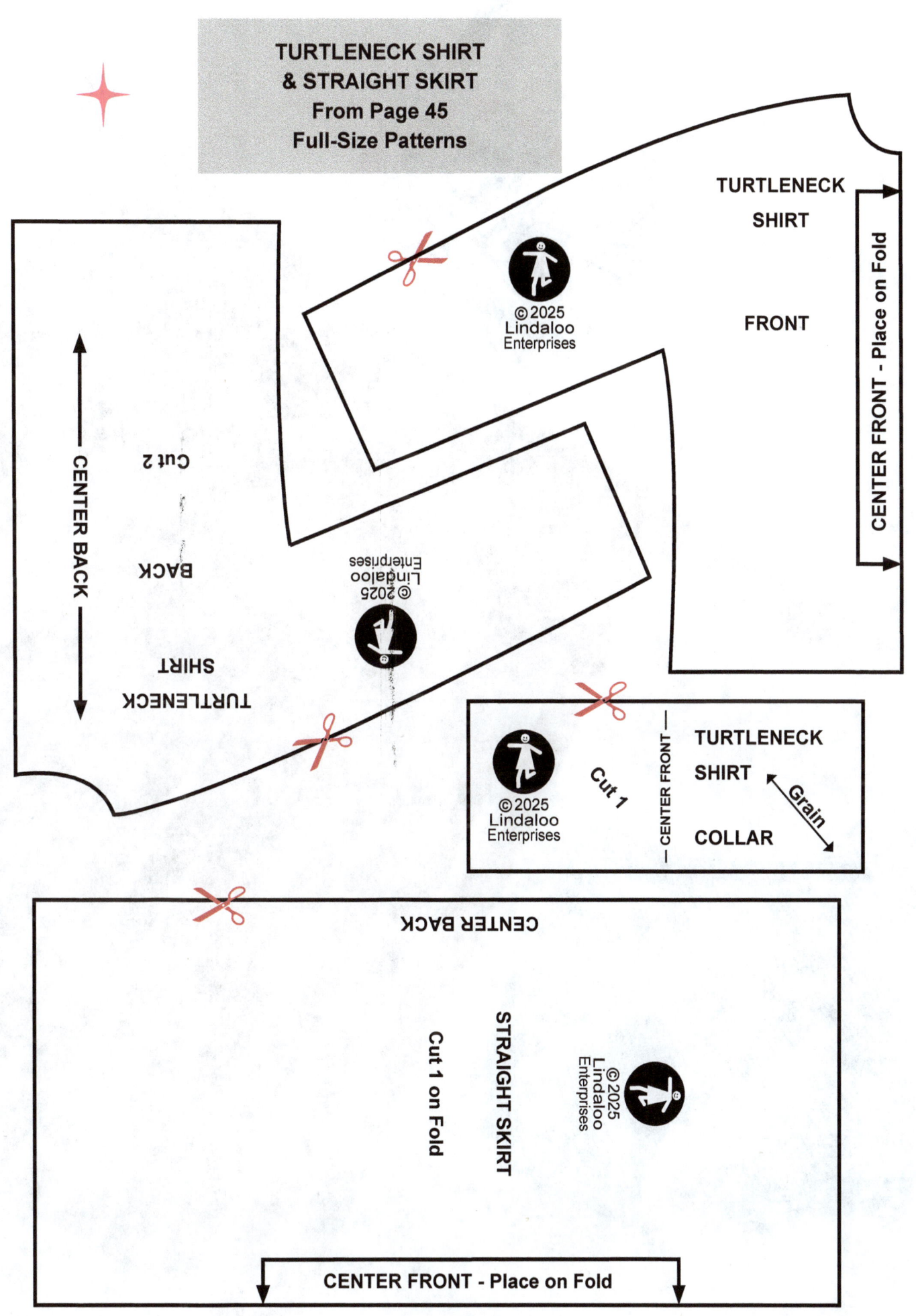

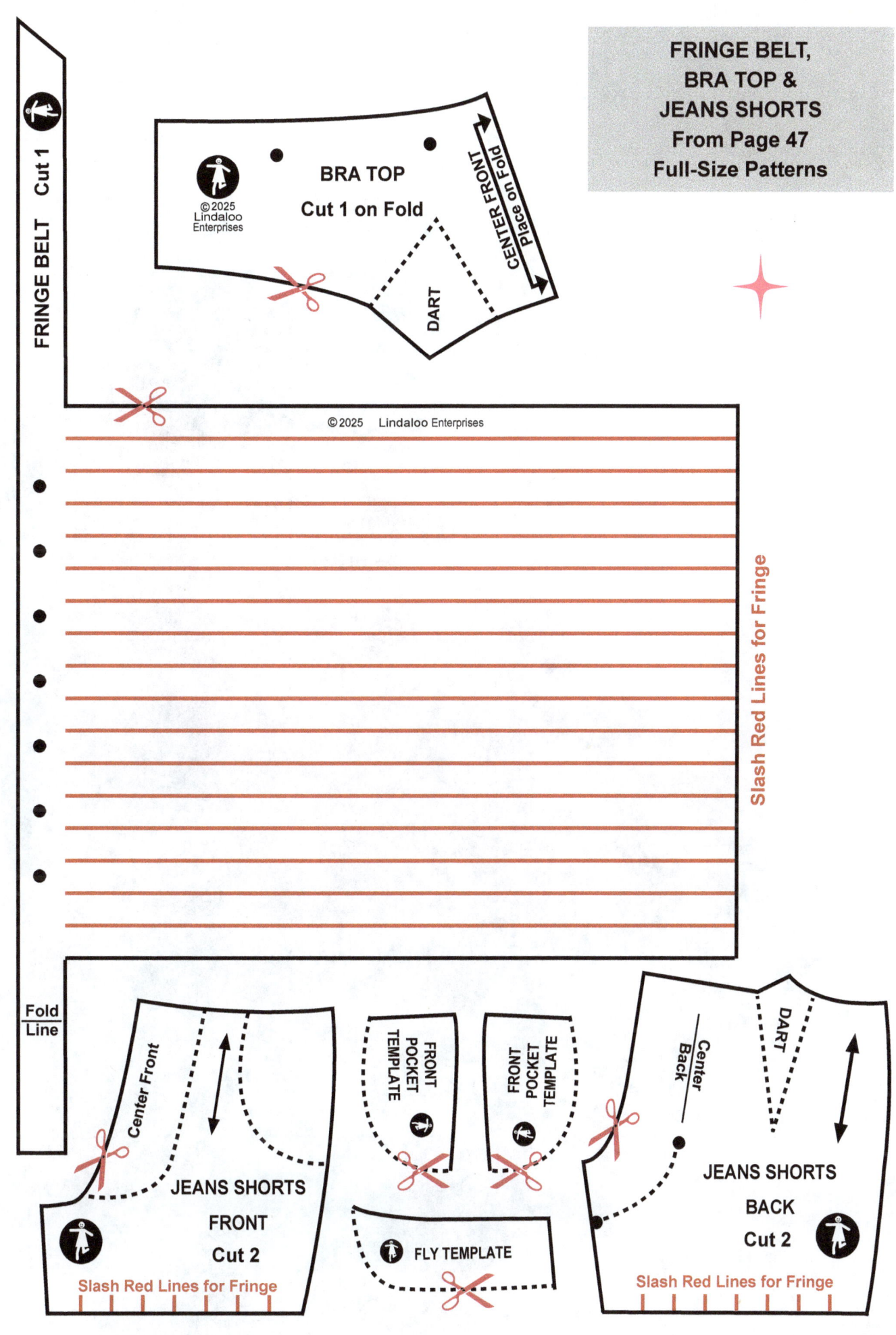

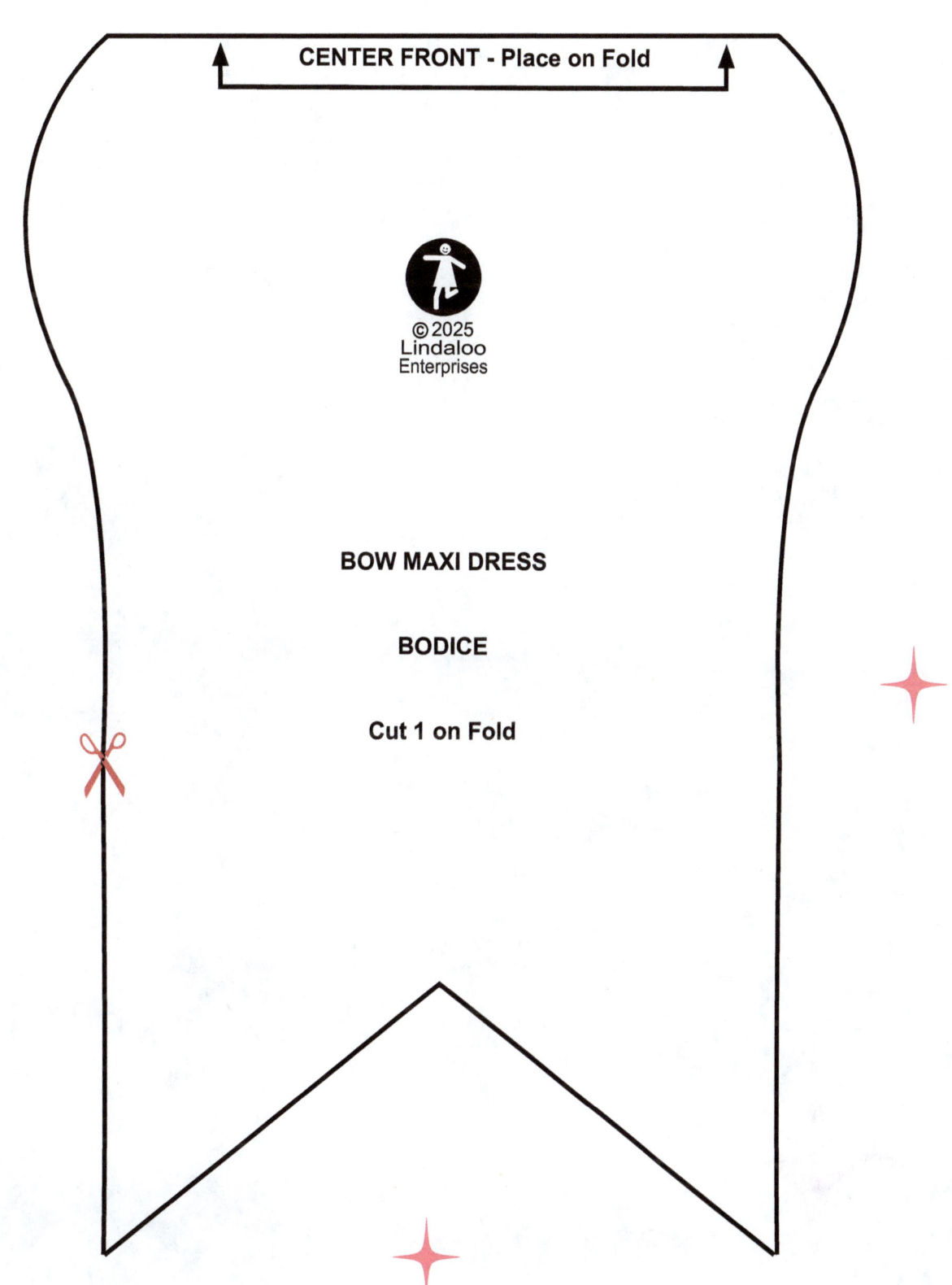

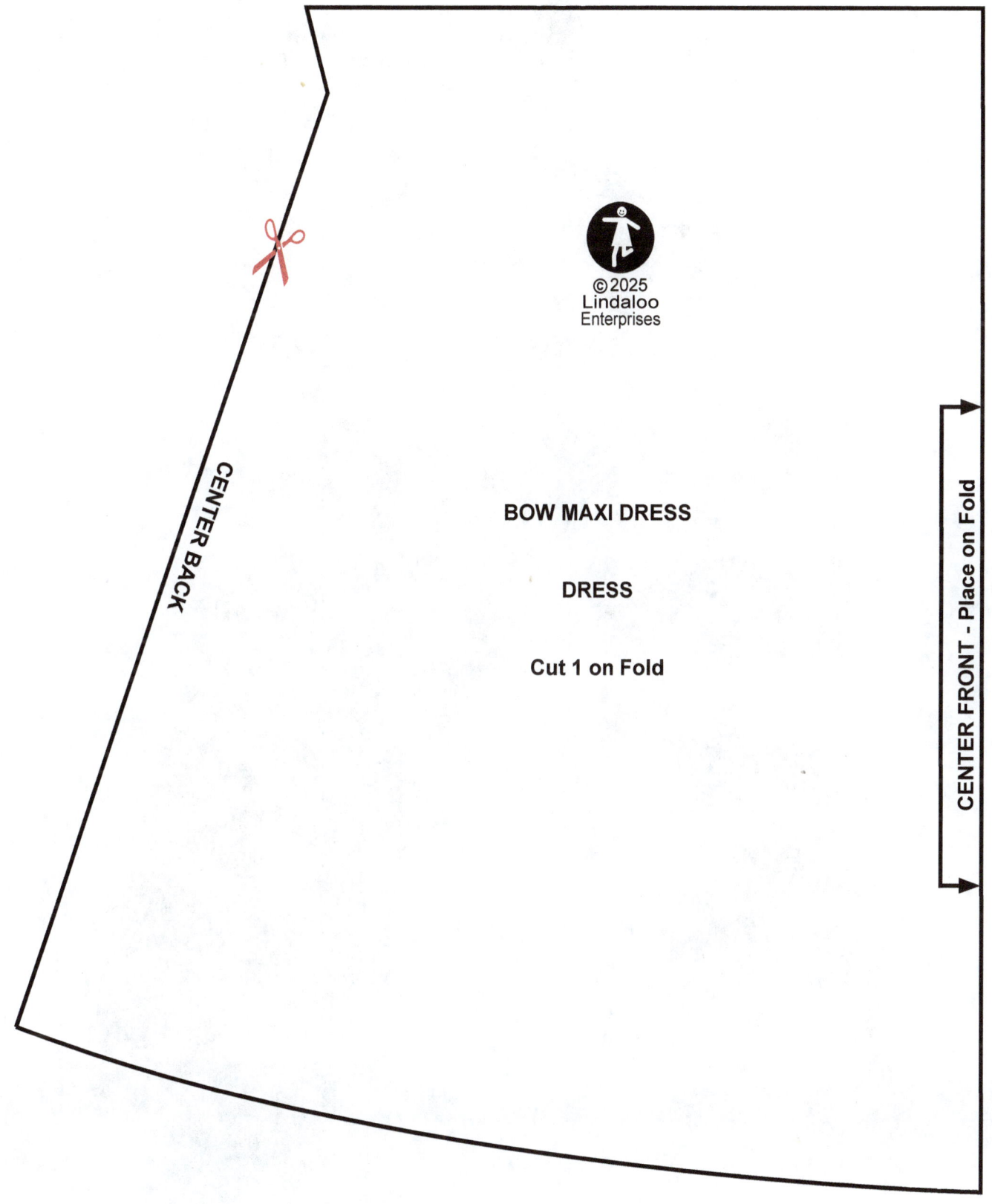

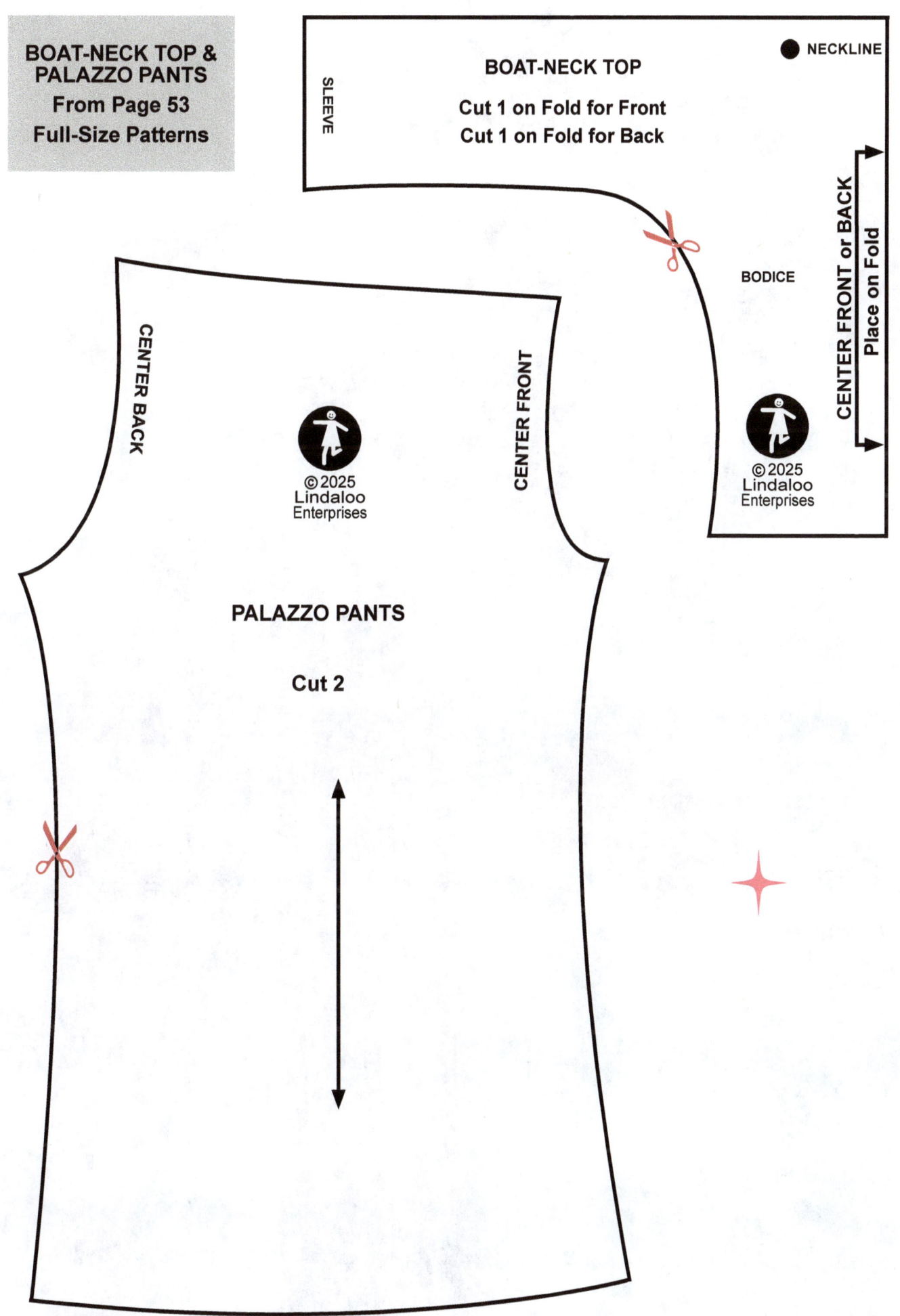

PART 1
PAJAMAS, SLIPPERS & SLEEP MASK
From Page 55
Full-Size Patterns

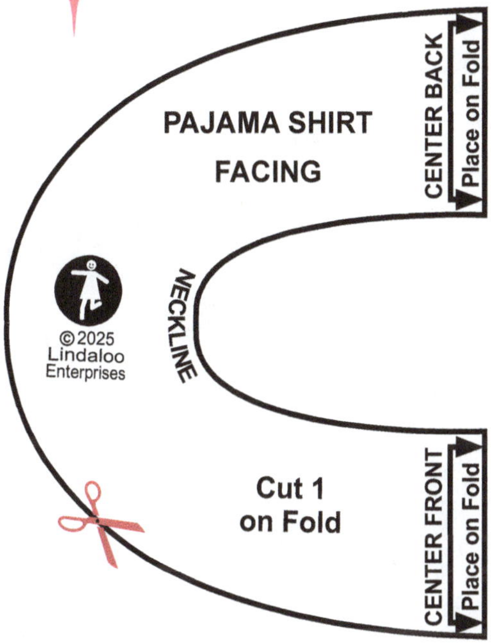

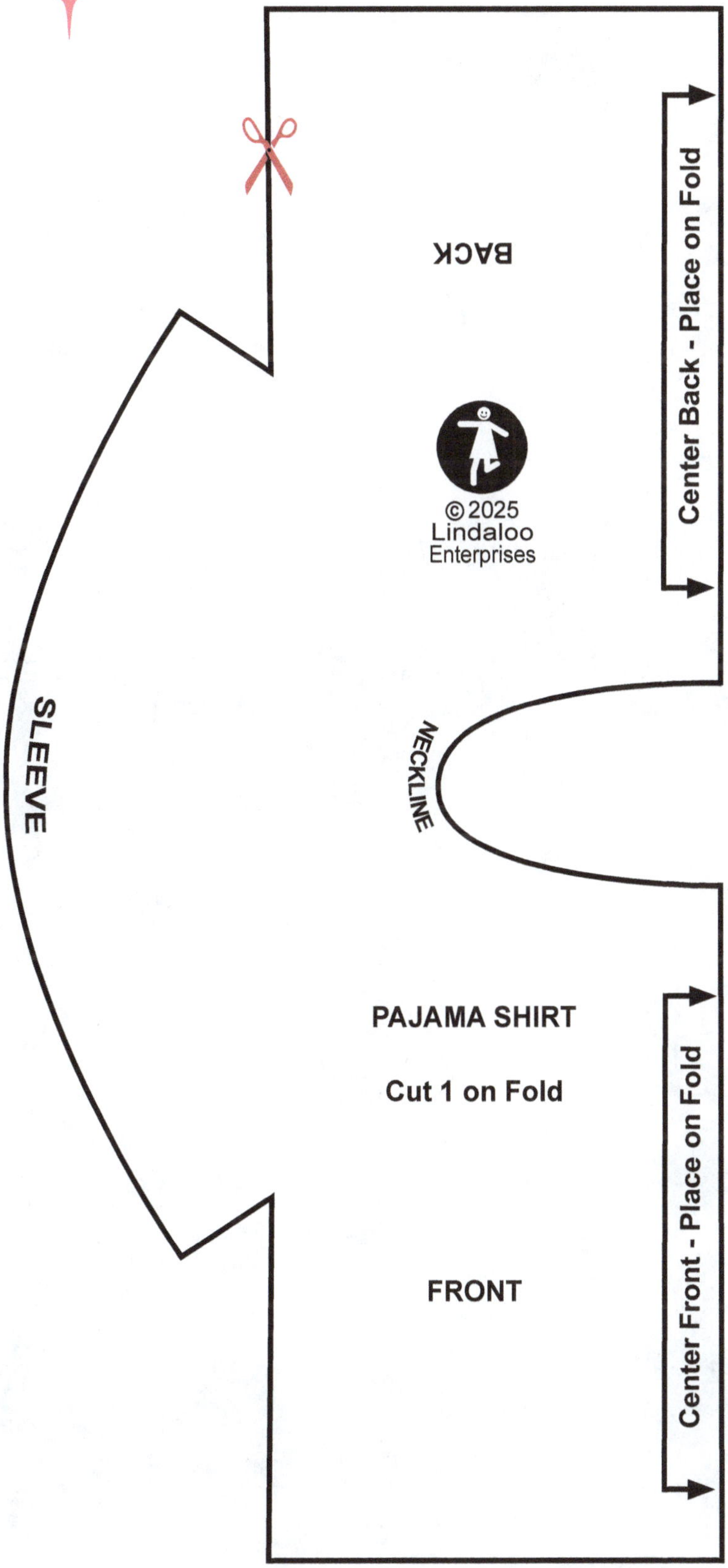

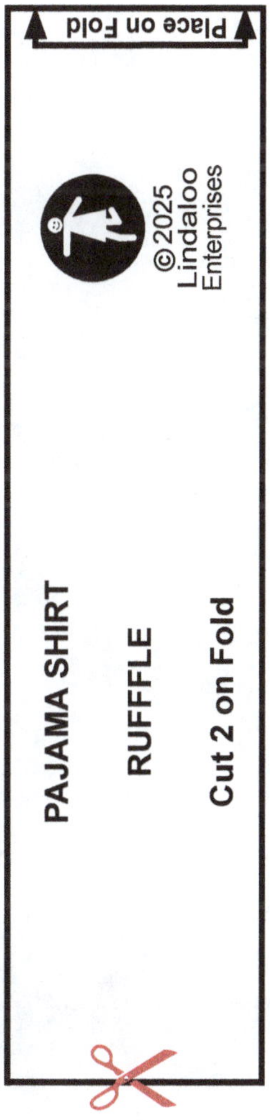

PAJAMA SHIRT FACING

NECKLINE

CENTER BACK - Place on Fold

CENTER FRONT - Place on Fold

Cut 1 on Fold

© 2025 Lindaloo Enterprises

BACK

Center Back - Place on Fold

SLEEVE

NECKLINE

PAJAMA SHIRT

Cut 1 on Fold

Center Front - Place on Fold

FRONT

© 2025 Lindaloo Enterprises

Place on Fold

PAJAMA SHIRT

RUFFFLE

Cut 2 on Fold

© 2025 Lindaloo Enterprises

PART 2
PAJAMAS, SLIPPERS & SLEEP MASK
From Page 55
Full-Size Patterns

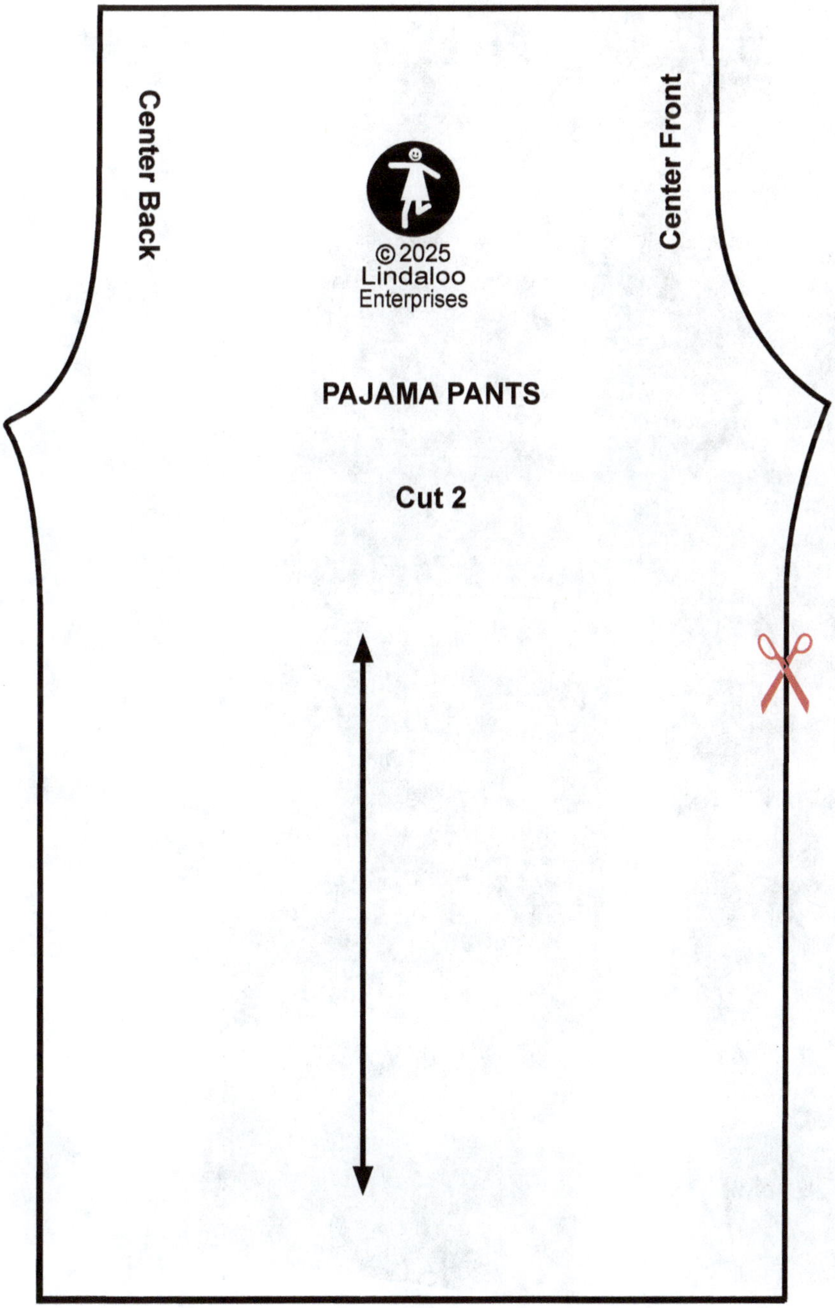

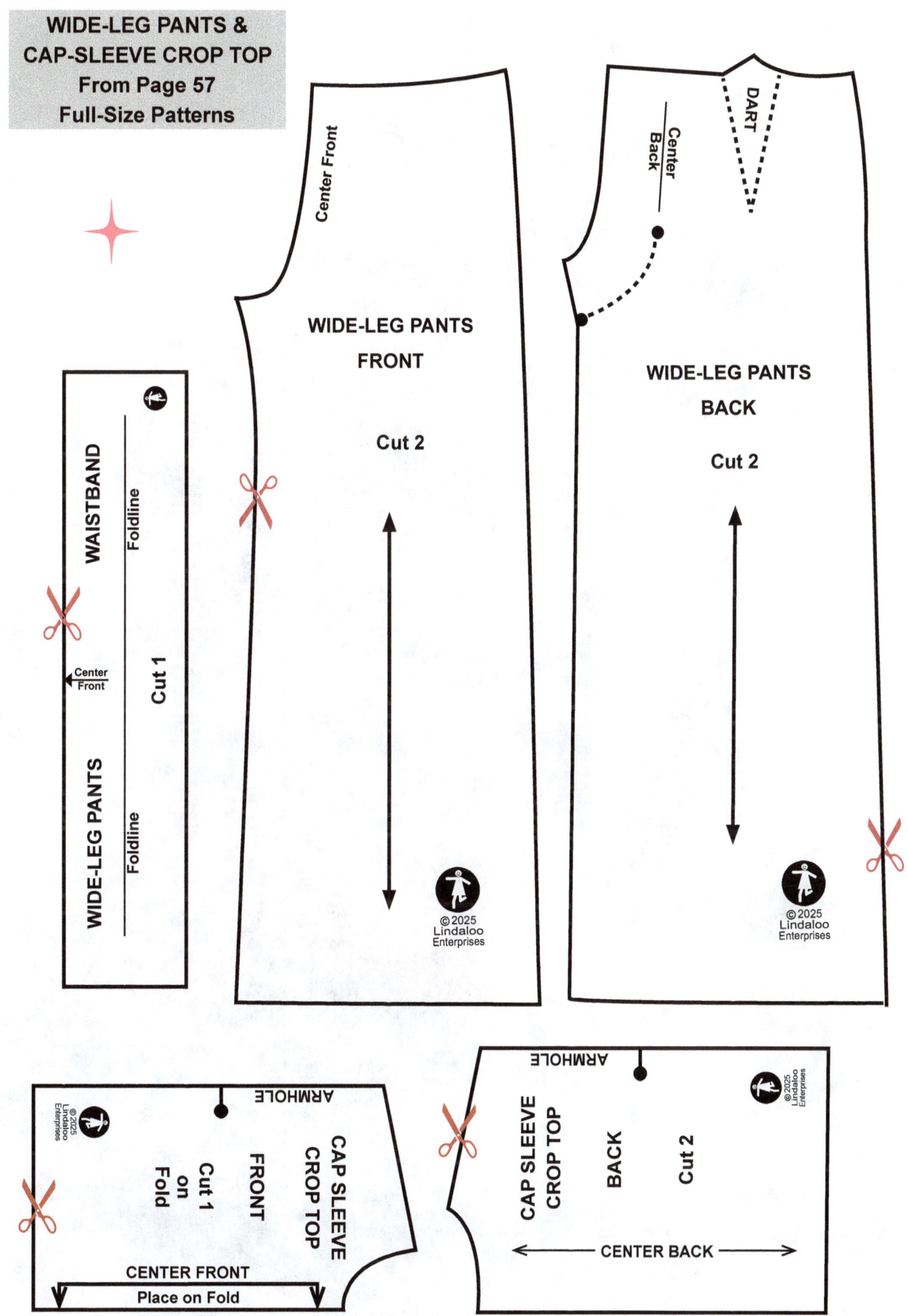

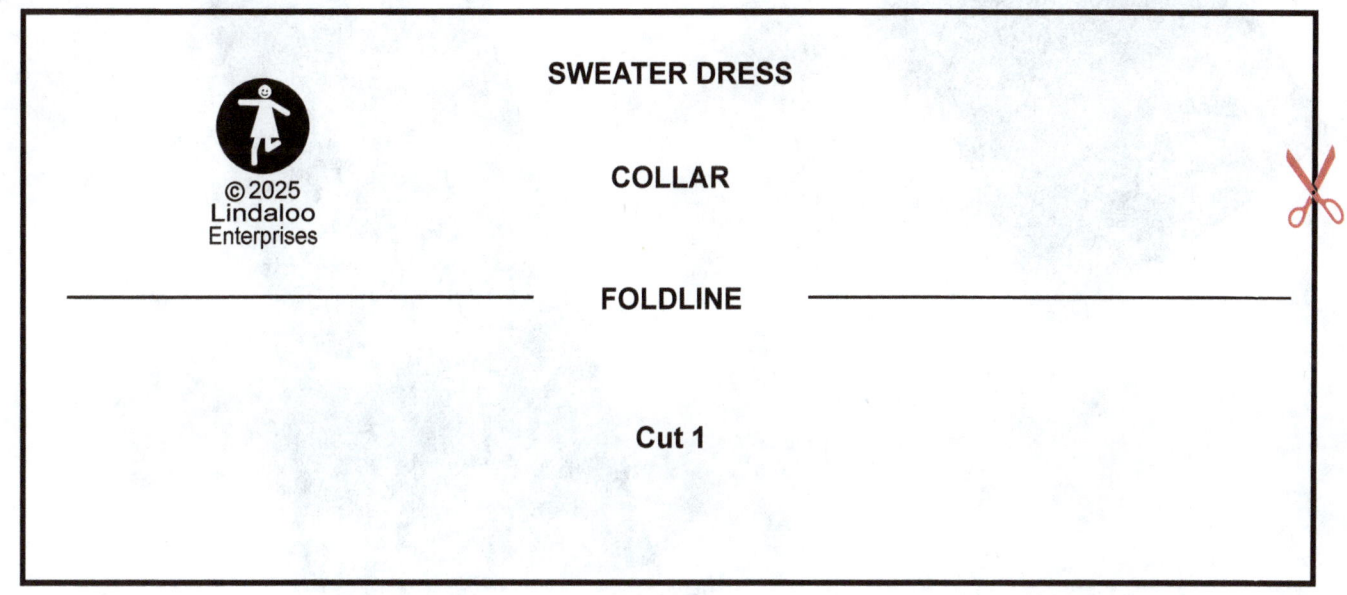

SWEATER DRESS & HAT
From Page 59
Full-Size Pattern for Dress
plus
Cutting Dimensions for Hat

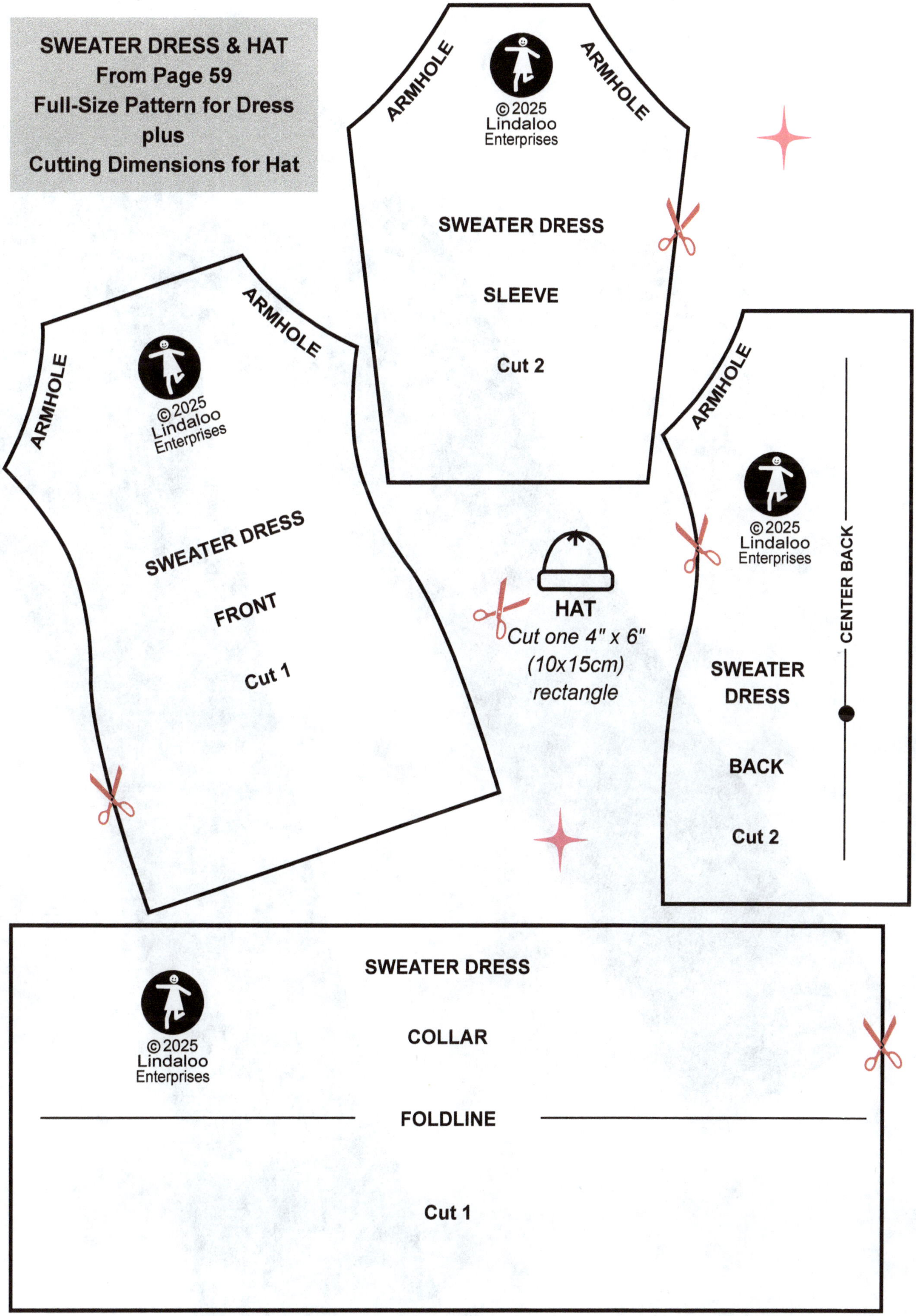

SWEATER DRESS SLEEVE — Cut 2

SWEATER DRESS FRONT — Cut 1

HAT — Cut one 4" x 6" (10x15cm) rectangle

SWEATER DRESS BACK — Cut 2 — CENTER BACK

SWEATER DRESS COLLAR — FOLDLINE — Cut 1

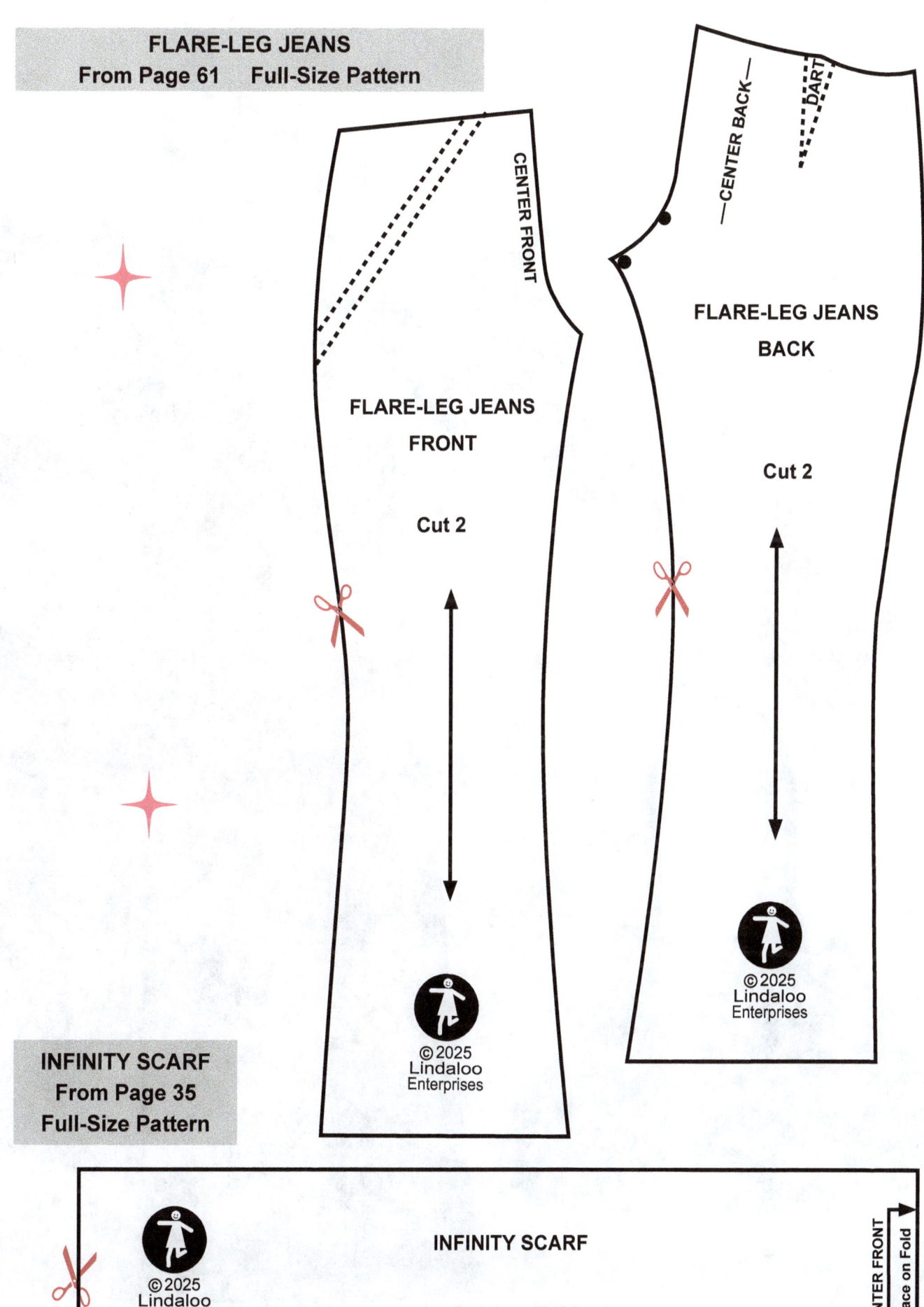

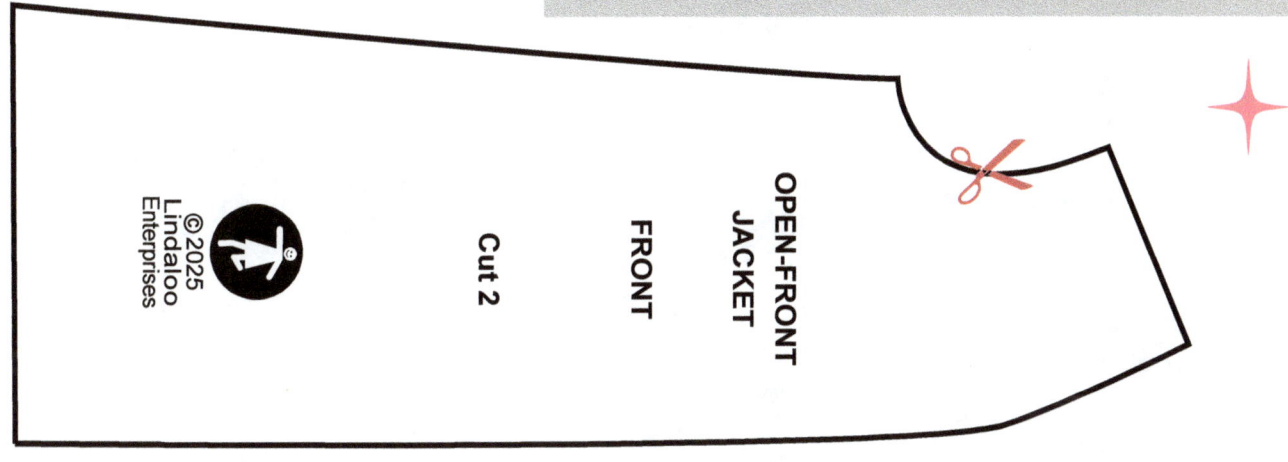

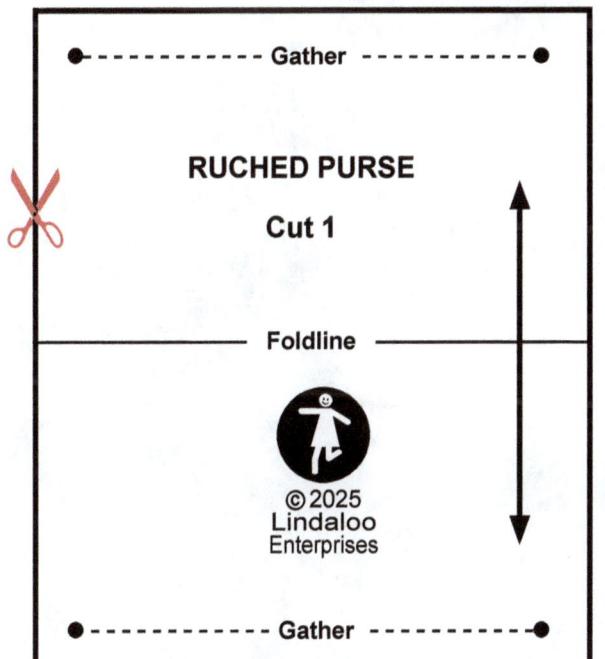
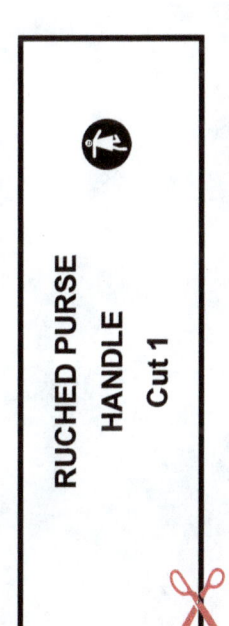

About the Author

LINDA WRIGHT studied textiles, patternmaking and clothing design at the Pennsylvania State University and has had a lifelong love of creating. She is the author of assorted handicraft books including doll clothes sewing patterns, amigurumi-style crochet, coloring books for grown-ups and her groundbreaking *Toilet Paper Origami*.

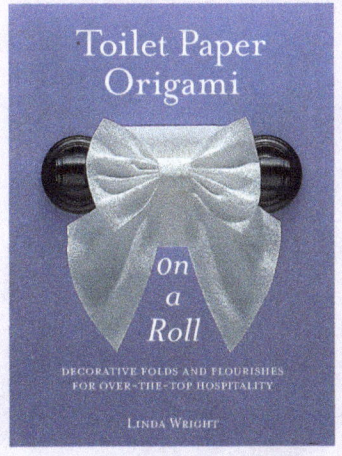

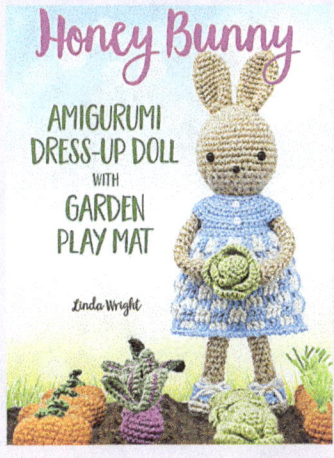

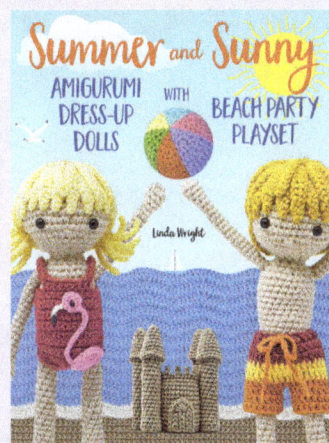

amazon.com/author/lindawright   pinterest.com/LindalooEnt   tiktok.com/@lindaloo_enterprises

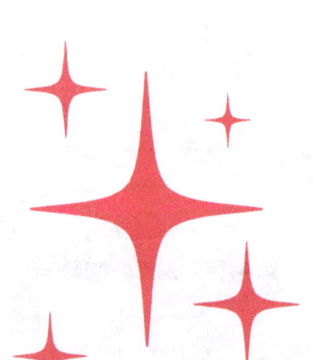

www.ingramcontent.com/pod-product-compliance
Lightning Source LLC
Chambersburg PA
CBHW080250170426
43192CB00014BA/2631